We Love Jenni

An Unauthorized Biography of Jenni Rivera

By **Marc Shapiro** (*NY Times* best-selling author)
with Charlie Vazquez

TABLE OF CONTENTS

THIS BOOK IS DEDICATED TO...

To my wife Nancy, thanks for the life and the love. To my daughter Rachael and granddaughter Lily, it's all good. Lori Perkins and Louise Fury, thanks for having my back. Riverdale Avenue Books, the next step in the great adventure. Mike Kirby, he's human. Charlie Vázquez, he's human. Brady and Fitch, they're dogs. To all the good the books, good music, and good art, the things that keep me up at night.

And finally, to Jenni Rivera. You had all the time in the world but ultimately not enough. What more can be said except rest in peace.

PREFACE

AND NOTHING BUT HE TRUTH

Less than twenty-four hours after Jenni Rivera's plane went down, I had a book deal in place to write a biography of Jenni Rivera. Sure, they wanted it sooner rather than later. Pop culture works at lightning speed, especially in the publishing business. You have to strike while the iron is hot—and every other cliché you can think of.

Books like this don't just get written on a whim (although occasionally that does happen). Some celebrity is in crisis or scandal? Write the book. Somebody new and hot on the scene? Write the book. And sadly, it is often the case that it is somebody whom people either know very well or don't know at all. Write the book.

Yes, I know it sounds very mercenary. Writing a book on a suddenly viable-in-death celebrity is part of the job of being a pop culture writer. The book does well, the author does well. The celebrity screw-ups think an hour of confessional time on Oprah Winfrey's couch is the first step in redemption in the public eye is kind of like that. The only difference is first they do

Oprah, then they write the book .

Are you listening, Lance Armstrong?

So if you're inclined, feel free to sling brickbats, F–bombs, and cries of "Exploitive grave-robber!" my way. I've got a thick hide. But if you've gotten this far, then you have a sense of discovery and curiosity about Jenni Rivera that you might have picked up from a sound bite on the nightly news. You might have heard her music blaring out of a car radio as you drove through town but did not have the time or inclination to match the music with the person. Hell, you might even have owned a Jenni Rivera CD or two but were not interested enough to delve beyond the songs. But that was then. Now you want to know everything. And for those willing to take the leap, Jenni's journey is a ticket to real-life high adventure.

For openers, it's a really a good story, full of drama and scandal and most importantly, a singer and her music that set the world, a culture, and a gender on a decidedly different course. Jenni was the whole package and, yes, she was decidedly human. Every time she figuratively stubbed her toe, something she seemed to do with regularity, she told us about it. No embarrassment was too great that Jenni did not take it to the widest possible public arena. That she survived it all with her integrity intact is a story in itself that was very much worth telling. And, oh yes, her zest for life, her spot-on business sense and heart the size of—well, you get the picture. Bottom line? Even if you didn't know Jenni, part of you probably feels like you should. Again, that's why you're here.

I knew a little about Jenni, thanks in large part to Elijah Wald's excellent book *Narcocorrido: A Journey into the Music of Drugs, Guns, and Guerrillas.* And thanks to my first-rate writing partner Charlie Vázquez, I learned quite a bit more on the fly . But like most gringos, going in I did not know much.

And therein lies the tragedy. We all discovered Jenni Rivera too late.

Jenni Rivera was never invisible. Nor was she flying below the radar. In a world of music-loving Mexican Americans, Jenni has been a star of massive proportions for quite a long time. At clubs and halls where Latin artists reigned supreme, the sound was big, brassy, and bold; the beer flowed freely; and a largely Mexican American audience could escape the reality of being, for the most part, at the bottom of the economic ladder . She was as well known as Adele and Barbra Streisand. If you lived in places like Lynwood, Paramount, East Los Angeles, and Monterrey, even more so. But to the man on the street of mainstream white-bread America, Jenni Rivera might as well have been from Mars or an inhabitant of a parallel universe.

Once the color line went from brown to white, it was, quite simply, *Jenni who*?

Her intended audience, the burgeoning Mexican American and immigrant population, found her early on. She spoke to them in a way that only they seemed to understand, although at the end of the day what she said was universal. Freedom. Empowerment. The right for women to be themselves. The desires that are not limited by race, religion, or how much you make.

The Latin media, in the U.S. and Mexico, was quick to tab her as the Next Big Thing and The Great Brown Hope. Whatever she did, be it major, minor, or just plain dramatic and scandalous, the likes of

Univision, *La Opinión*, and Reforma were all over it. Here in the States? Well, that was a whole other story.

With very rare exception, most of the major English-language newspapers looked the other way even as her record sales soared into the millions. Ironically the biggest splash Jenni made in the English media was the day the *Los Angeles Times* ran a gushy news item in their real estate section on how Jenni had recently purchased a $3 million house in the Valley. To more than one cynical observer, the reason they did that story was that, by having that kind of money and making that kind of purchase, she was now acting white.

Okay, enough of the rant. You get the picture.

But Jenni was persistent. She was inching closer to the gold ring after more than a decade in the trenches. With a network sitcom in the very serious development stage and her first all-English-language and very radio-friendly pop album set for release, this book may well have been written for a different reason in about a year—to celebrate a success rather than to remember the long eventful journey to a life cut short.

If, if, if. You can make yourself crazy behind that word. But 'if' things had been different—well, we'll never know.

Things went along this way until the day Jenni died. Then the U.S. media that had largely denied her existence were suddenly put in the position of playing catch-up, consulting every Mexican journalist and professor of Latino studies they could find to help them make sense of Jenni. And I'm not leaving myself out of this loop. I was right there with the best of them, trying to find the answer to just what made Jenni

Rivera tick.

And what made Jenni Rivera so damned important.

It's too late to undo the slight that has been done. But it's not too late to tell the story.

- Marc Shapiro 2013

PROLOGUE

TIME TO SAY GOODBYE

December 2, 2012. Texcoco, Mexico.

Corrido singing star Lupillo Rivera was putting the finishing touches on a show that had already gone into the early hours of the morning. He had been a music star in this part of the world for some time. He knew the ropes of being a star. Not a whole lot surprised him.

As Lupillo was about to launch into another song, a raucous explosion of shouts and cheers cut through the night. Lupillo had been receiving this kind of response all night but he most likely sensed that something different was in the air. Instinctively he looked offstage—

—just as his sister, Jenni Rivera, walked out on

stage.

The tearful, emotional reunion that followed was seven years in the making. Jenni and Lupillo had an alleged falling out, but nobody seemed to remember why. Their respective careers had kept them constantly on the go—careers that, by degrees, were moving in divergent ways, and in many quarters it was said that Jenni's career had eclipsed that of her brother's. Jenni would be the first one to tell you it was never a big deal until the media made it that way. What was known was that they had not been together for any length of time and that those moments were tense and those seven years had been far from perfect for two people for whom family was uppermost. Brother and sister hugged on stage, drank a tequila toast, and then sang Jenni's song "Ya lo sé". The song was powerful and emotional. It had always meant something. At this moment, it meant something more.

"I just came back to give him so much that he has given to me since I was a little girl," she said in a *Billboard* news report. "Although we have had our family differences, he knows how much I love him."

***

The Rivera family was close. They were there for all the special occasions, the good times and the bad times. And it was not an uncommon sight to see Jenni Rivera receiving well wishes, hugs, and kisses from a family member as she was about to board a plane on her way to another show or round of promotion for her latest album. Like any true traditional Mexican send-off, there was always a lot of emotion when a Rivera was saying good-bye. It was deep and real when the Rivera family separated. Although they were believers in good health and long life, there was something ingrained in their psyches and religious beliefs that made every goodbye seem like it might be the last.

It was one of those days during the first week in December when Jenni was set to fly out of Los Angeles and head to Mexico for a series of concerts. Jenni had much on her plate at the moment and it would have been easy to postpone those shows for another time. But Jenni was nothing if not loyal to the people who helped get her to the pinnacle of stardom. And she could not argue with the fact that the people of Mexico had certainly aided her in her climb to the top.

So she was standing at the foot of the gangway, preparing to board the plane.

Her brother, Pedro Rivera Jr., was on hand to see her off. Her brother was a pastor in Iglesia Primer Amor, a church in Whittier, California. Besides being a religious man, he was also a highly intuitive one . On that day, his feelings about his sister caused him some concern.

"I had a feeling that something was going to happen," he told CNS. "So I hugged her and kissed her goodbye."

On Friday, December 7, her brother Juan said goodbye as well. He texted her with a simple message. "Sister I Love You."

CHAPTER ONE

THE HOURS

Jenni Rivera loved to Tweet and text.

She had embraced the new technology with the same passion as she had her music. It was the rare moment when she did not have her cell phone in her hand and was tapping out a message on her keypad to family, friends, or her multitude of fans in the Twitterverse. Jenni just loved to be in touch. It was just the way she was.

On December 7, 2012, the message was a photo of the "Diva of Banda" holding up a sign in Spanish. It read *"Nos vemos este 7 en Colima, 8 en Monterrey."* Literally translated, it was a simple update of her itinerary.

"See you the 7th in Colima. 8 in Monterrey."

December 8, 2012:

It seemed like a good day to fly.

That's how Jenni Rivera and her entourage felt as they Tweeted and talked excitedly amongst themselves and posed giddily and mugged for cell phone photos as they awaited their noon departure at Toluca International Airport, just outside of Mexico City. The superstar singer and her traveling party—publicist

Arturo Rivera, attorney Mario Macias, hair stylist Jorge Sánchez, and makeup artist Jacob Yenbale—had long ago gotten used to the idea of traveling on commercial airlines, but today they were like little children at the possibility of finally flying on a private jet—a Learjet 25, which was parked on the airport tarmac.

This was contrary to Jenni's feelings a couple of months earlier when she told her good friend and Univision reporter Raul De Molina that she sensed she was traveling too much. De Molina recalled the interview in a *Colorlines* feature. "She told me that I'm putting my life at risk every weekend, traveling so much. I don't want to keep presenting myself at all these places because I don't know what is going to happen."

But as she prepared to fly into Monterrey, any fear had apparently been replaced by excitement. She liked the idea of flying in a Learjet so much that she was seriously thinking of buying the plane when this current jaunt was completed.

The good cheer continued during the plane's short hop to Monterrey. Her December 9 show at the 18,000-seat Monterrey Arena had been sold out for three weeks. Gustavo López, executive vice president of Universal Music Latin Entertainment, Jenni's parent music label, and also her close friend, related that he placed an urgent phone call to Jenni that Saturday. Some close friends who lived in Monterrey had been unable to buy tickets. Jenni said it was no problem and she secured passes for his friends. Typical of Jenni; "No Problem" was her mantra.

But her good cheer went much further than that,

for Jenni Rivera was about to crack the big time.

Her first substantial film role, "Filly Brown", opposite veteran actor Edward James Olmos, was set to open nationally in the United States in the coming year, and word on the street was that her portrayal of a drug-addicted, incarcerated mother of a budding hip-hop singer was already getting a groundswell of Oscar buzz. Her latest album, "Joyas Prestadas", already certified gold and closing in on platinum in Mexico, was to be released the following week in the U.S. And the consensus among music industry pundits was that the pop version of the album might just be the final key in unlocking the door to the massive U.S. market. Her work as a judge and mentor on the television show *The Voice: Mexico* continued to draw raves. Her children were healthy and happy. Even her recent divorce from her third husband, Major League Baseball pitcher Esteban Loaiza, could not dampen her spirits.

"I feel very blessed," she would tell the assembled press, that included Univision and *Qué Más* later that night. "I'm a very fortunate woman. I can't believe the things that have happened in my life."

The plane touched down in Monterrey in mid-afternoon. As she drove past the Monterrey Arena, Jenni was heartened by the fact that fans were already beginning to gather outside the arena, hours before her scheduled performance.

It was going to be a good night.

Jenni's enthusiasm for the response afforded by her fans in Monterrey was so great that during her sound check for the night's performance, she informed promoter Jesús Arreola that she would love to come back and do another show in February.

During the hours leading up to the performance, Jenni was her typical outgoing, congenial self: socializing with friends, record company types, and fellow performers who were there to see Jenni do her magic. One of those was reigning pop diva Alejandra Guzmán. According to a report filed by *El Diario*, the pair got along so famously that at one point Jenni invited the singer to join them on their post-show flight back to Mexico City and, subsequently, to do a performance together during her taping of *The Voice Mexico*.

Backstage at the Monterrey Arena, Jenni was going through her pre-concert rituals, final touches on her hair and makeup. Then, as reported by *Qué Más*, her last chore before going onstage was to text her youngest son, 11-year-old Johnny Ángel López, an indication that the welfare of her children was uppermost in her thoughts.

The arena went dark and just as suddenly was bathed in hypnotic bursts of light. Jenni's backing band struck traditional chords and musical bombast. The crowd exploded into wild applause and cheers. It was show time.

What had long been referred to as "The Jenni Rivera Experience" was a rousing success, full of her trademark emotionally charged songs, several costume changes, and a realistic presentation of the power and passion that had made Jenni a true star. Jenni liked to do things her way. It was why there was rarely an opening act. It was also not uncommon for a Jenni show to run in excess of three hours in length.

At one point in the concert, a representative of Jenni's record company stepped on stage and presented the astonished singer with a gold record award for "Joyas Prestadas" as the crowd cheered.

Jenni was at her best but, as more than one reporter noted, that night she did seem a bit tired. Stardom had its price and Jenni was most certainly burning the proverbial candle at both ends: first and foremost as mother, then singer, recording artist, reality television star, and shortly, as a final step in breaking big in the all-important U.S. market, the upcoming all-English-language album and a development deal with U.S. television for a primetime show. She had made the acquaintance of another Long Beach native, rapper Snoop Dogg, and they were in serious talks to do a song together. Jenni was also thinking answering the notion that her life would make a good book and, until recently, she had been working on her autobiography.

The increased interest in Jenni had gone international. Whereas her primary performing territories had been Mexico, Los Angeles, and pockets in the Southwest and Midwest, Jenni was now getting offers from Spain, Columbia, El Salvador, and Honduras. In a case of art imitating life, Jenni had remarked in an episode of her reality series *I Love Jenni* that she did not want to take the new offers, that her career had gotten out of control and that she was thinking about retiring and just being with her kids.

But lost in the rush of "projects" was the fact that Jenni had arrived, at forty-three years of age, as a true pioneer of Mexican music and of women's empowerment, particularly in the Mexican community. She had singlehandedly turned the traditional "hardcore" conceit of male-dominated music—and in particular traditional *corridos*, *norteños*, and, more recently, *narcocorridos*—with tough music from a woman's perspective. She was a driving force in the current push by Latina women for equal rights and equality in the non-music world. Stereotypes and preconceived notions as they pertained to Latina women were falling like hay at the business end of an axe. Jenni was a creative and emotional blade wielded in mighty fashion through her music and her mere presence in the public arena.

This was a lot on the plate for somebody who, despite being born and raised in America and selling millions of albums and selling out endless concerts, was little more than a marginal blip on the pop culture landscape in the U.S. The lion's share of the coverage of Jenni in the States had been largely in the domain of Spanish-language media with the very rare English language outlet. And sadly, what little coverage she was getting usually focused on the much publicized scandal and drama in her life. If a new album came out, she might get a mention in *Billboard* or *People en Español*. But if a relationship went bad, or she punched out a fan, or when yes, a sex tape emerged, the press on both sides of the border was all over it like tabloid sharks.

Ironically, the singer continued to remain primarily an unknown quantity in the U.S.— and, for that matter, in most of the rest of the world.

Elijah Wald, an author/music historian who interviewed Jenni and the entire Rivera clan in 1998 for his groundbreaking look at the history of hardcore Mexican music *Narcocorrido: A Journey into the Music of Drugs, Guns, and Guerrillas*, told this author in a 2012 interview that he would be shocked if any of the singer's reported 15 million albums sold were bought by somebody who was not Mexican. "I would be surprised if there were a lot of people who didn't speak Spanish buying those records. "

Wald also acknowledged that outside her home base in Los Angeles, the reported national tours were highly exaggerated. "She was not particularly visible nationally. There were pockets in the southwest, like Phoenix, Arizona, where she would have appeared and I'm certain there were places in the U.S. where the records were selling. But even when she was selling out four-thousand-seat rooms in places like the Kodak Theater in Los Angeles, she was not really well known outside of Los Angeles."

While acknowledging Jenni's contributions and her arrival as a superstar on the Mexican music scene, the ever-candid Wald said that, like most superstars, Jenni remained a polarizing personality even in the Mexican community.

"Anyone who considered themselves hip hated Jenni. She was very much a working-class woman's phenomena. To nice girls she was considered gross and ugly. She completely split people."

But while largely unknown in most of the world, on this night in Monterrey, Mexico, she was a superstar.

It was the rare observation that did not compare Jenni to another Latin performer, Selena, whose greatness and, most importantly, inroads into English language stardom were cut short by a bullet. Many, including author Wald, have likened Jenni to a Dolly Parton type: somebody whose persona carried as much weight as her music. But even those critics less inclined to praise saw Jenni as carrying the banner for Mexican culture and, perhaps more importantly, the empowerment of Mexican women who had long suffered because of entrenched male-dominated tradition.

But even flag bearers get tired and on that night, Jenni most certainly was.

However, while tired, her after-concert press conference was both energetic and vintage Jenni. She was jovial, openly grateful for her successes, and as informal and unpretentious as any star could possibly be. It was not an uncommon practice to pepper her remarks to reporters with "honey" and

"sweetie." It closed the often huge divide between celebrities and the media. And like every other encounter with the press, the reporters were like putty in her hands at this post-concert press conference.

The questions were largely softballs but the occasional tough question was also asked and Jenni had no trouble answering it.

The singer had worn her troubled hard-knocks life on her sleeve and in her music for years and she had shown a capacity for not dodging any questions. When a sex tape of herself and a former boyfriend hit the Internet, she was front and center in talking about it rather than denying it. When scandal erupted regarding the charge that her oldest daughter, Janney, had slept with her third husband (a charge denied by her daughter), she did not shy away from the tabloid questions. Her father's infidelity that produced a half-brother and ultimately the divorce of her parents? She was angry and she said so . And so alternately funny and serious, that night she addressed her recent third divorce, this one from former Major League Baseball player Esteban Loazia, as well as questions geared toward recent developments in her career.

In comments ultimately picked up by CNN, NBC Latino, and countless other world media outlets, Jenni said, "I'm tired and want to spend the holidays with my family. But only God knows what will happen." During the interview she also waxed philosophical on the question of the negativity in her life. "I can't get up in the negative which destroys you. I have brothers. I have children. I have nephews. They keep me from focusing on the negative."

The singer also took the opportunity to paint herself as every woman. "I am a woman like any other and ugly things happen to me like any other women. The number of times I have fallen down is the number of times I have gotten up."

One comment during the press conference effectively summed up where Jenni Rivera had come from and where she was going. "I want more and I'm always looking for it."

Later that evening, the show's promoters offered to put Jenni and her entourage up in an elegant suite for the night. In fact, promoter Jesús Arreola told *Conexión Total* that, in anticipation of her staying the night, "We had four tables in the VIP area set up for her and we had her disguise ready for her so no one would recognize her. We also had a hotel reserved for her."

But at two thirty a.m., the promoter received a call from Jenni and her people, thanking him for his hospitality but that "Jenni had changed her plans and that they would be flying out right away to Toluca."

On any other occasion Jenni would have graciously accepted the hospitality. But Jenni declined that night, reasoning that it would be easier to fly back to Mexico City at night and get some sleep before traveling to nearby Toluca to tape an episode of *The Voice: Mexico*. The extra time would also give her the opportunity for a few days' rest before continuing her Mexico concert tour with appearances in Michoacan and Chiapas.

According to *El Diario*, Jenni and Alejandra Guzmán did not connect after the show and Guzmán would ultimately wind up spending the night in Monterrey.

It was with a mixture of exhaustion and adrenaline-fueled excitement that Jenni and her party returned to the Monterrey airport and their waiting Learjet. Shortly after entering the plane, the group mugged for a cell phone photo taken by one of the pilots. Reportedly the pilot sent the photo to his mother but that could not ultimately be proven. What is known is that the photo was later discovered on makeup artist Yenbale's Instagram account. It showed Jenni and her people smiling happily for the photo. A caption under the photo, written by Yenbale, said, "We getting back to Mexico City. Jenni, Rivera, Arturo, Gigi and Me. Los Amool!"

At 3:05 a.m., the Learjet began to taxi down the runway. Jenni texted one more time. It was not known to whom. The Learjet lurched into the early morning night.

Ten minutes later, the plane disappeared off control tower radar.

CHAPTER TWO

COMING TO AMERICA

Don Pedro Rivera was born in Jalisco in Western Mexico. Rosa Saavedra was born in Sonora in Northern Mexico. These were not the best of times to be from either place.

Especially if you had designs on living a long life.

The tiny villages that dotted much of the Mexican countryside during the '50s and into the '60s were hotbeds of lawlessness, hopelessness, and rampant poverty. The last bastion of the wild frontier, Jalisco and Sonora were known for the poverty of its people, a place where family feuds often erupted into gunfights and the burgeoning drug smuggling trade was both a source of employment and, just as often, the cause of violent death.

It was within an environment of often violent and dangerous surroundings that a very romantic story unfolded, according to a conversation Jenni had early in her career with *Open Your Eyes* magazine.

"What's really cool and ironic was that my mother was 15," she said. "His father was in the military and so he wasn't around much and so he would spend a couple of weeks with his family and then he would be gone the rest of the year."

She further related that on one such trip, her father rode his bicycle from Jalisco all the way to Sonora, where he got a job selling lottery tickets at a local restaurant in nearby Hermosillo. "One night, the restaurant was having a singing contest. My mom was singing and my father instantly fell in love with her and her voice."

Rosa Saavedra saw few options in life, as did most young women growing up at the time. Marriage and children was the most any would hope for. But Rosa was known around her village as somebody with a good singing voice, which was why Rosa would often exercise the fantasy of a better life by singing in amateur singing competitions set up by local restaurants.

In looking back years later on her parents' courtship, Jenni jokingly told *Aquí y Ahora,* "He robbed her, as they would say back then."

Don Pedro was an honorable man who knew the right thing to do when he met the woman of his dreams was to marry her, make babies, and try to carve a little bit of heaven out of the hell that was their surroundings.

With marginal education and few marketable skills, prospects for any kind of life were limited, and for Pedro and Rosa, married and with two sons by late 1966, their future looked bleak.

Don Pedro had heard the stories about the possibilities that lay just across the border. Possibilities of a better life . Rosa and Don Pedro discussed their options. They were few.

It was then that they decided that their only hope for a better life lay across the border—in the United States.

Don Pedro would later recall in a *Los Angeles Times* interview that the people who were leaving Mexico for the United States "had either killed someone, the government was looking for them, or they were very poor. The U.S. was their refuge."

Don Pedro would make an exploratory trip to the United States on his own in 1966. He would end up in Culver City, California, where he found a United States that, despite a cultural and social revolution in the '60s that emphasized freedom and equal rights, was less than hospitable, he said in an interview with *Hogar al Día*. "When I arrived in Culver City, I was seeing signs in restaurants that said 'No Animals, Negros, or Mexicans' allowed. It was very hard, very difficult."

It was all very new to Don Pedro. But having been largely on his own from an early age had served him well. There were some anxious moments as he set out in this brave new world. But his rugged individualism and confidence masked any notion of fear.

Don Pedro laid down some semblance of roots, then returned to Mexico in 1968. The family began what would be an arduous trek across the desert that led to the U.S./Mexico border. The going was rough, with savage heat during the day and frigid cold at night, a trip all the more challenging because Rosa was now pregnant with a third child. Rosa would later recall in a 2001 interview chronicled by *The Huffington Post* that at one point she had considered aborting the pregnancy but her religious beliefs pushed her to continue the pregnancy.

Years later, Jenni would reflect in a *Billboard Magazine* interview about her mother telling her how she was almost not born. "They came to this country to give my brothers a better life and here they were, pregnant with me. My mom was very honest when she told me, 'I tried all kinds of home remedies for you not to be born,' but that I refused to exit her body. "

Rosa's faith was rewarded when the couple and their children crossed the border and settled in the seaside town of Long Beach, California, a stretch of low-income property and tumble-down apartments and houses that most certainly must have reminded them of the poverty they had fled in Mexico. It was a neighborhood that Jenni would lovingly refer to as "the barrio". Gang problems were a constant in the area of Hill Street and Gale Avenue. Fights between warring factions and gunshots in the night were common and largely taken for granted.

Jenni's brother, Lupillo, remembered the rough-and-tumble side of their neighborhood in a conversation with author Elijah Wald. "People were getting killed every two or three hours. Not every day; every two or three hours somebody would get shot."

Jenni saw her neighborhood in a more rose-colored glasses way.

"It was a nice neighborhood," she told the *OC Weekly*, "but it was a ghetto neighborhood but a diverse neighborhood. Our friends were Samoans, Filipinos, blacks, all races."

The Mexican communities were a study in transition. Populated largely by immigrants, areas in

Lynwood, Paramount, Pico Rivera, and Long Beach reflected the true Mexican roots. These arrivals brought with them their lifestyles, religion, and all the hopes and dreams that led them to come to America. But the dreams of riches beyond belief were quickly dashed by the reality. The bias against Mexicans was culpable. Jobs were scarce. Reasonably paying or minimum-wage jobs were even harder to find.

Looking back on those early years, it was all a happy blur of sights and sounds for Jenni. "We lived as many immigrant families did," she recalled in a comprehensive interview with *Aquí y Ahora*. "We lived economically limited, but always happy."

Years later, Jenni's father, Don Pedro, would reflect in a conversation with Channel 62 News that the Rivera family got along in their new world by getting along. "We were a very quiet, discreet people," he said. "We never offended anybody."

Don Pedro was quick to embrace their new home. Driven and ambitious, he soon found work in Los Angeles factories as a plastics worker and as a bartender. He would occasionally earn extra money shooting memento photos for bar patrons. But while he wholeheartedly embraced America, Pedro had brought much of the memories of Jalisco and Sonora with him. He possessed a very good singing voice, and Rosa and the children would often listen, amused and also impressed when Don Pedro would spontaneously break into song—emotional *norteño* ballads reflecting those tough times and the realities that had brought them to America.

Two days short of Independence Day, July 2, 1969, Jenny Dolores Rivera Saavedra was born in a

Culver City, California, hospital. The family would finally grow to five children with the subsequent births of Gustavo and Rosie who, along with Jenni, Lupillo, and Juan, made for a literal full house.

Jenni's parents were thrilled to have a daughter. But, perhaps more importantly, they were aware that Jenni was a firstborn Mexican-American and the advantages and possibilities of being born in the United States would be better for her than for her parents and older brothers. Citizenship had its advantages.

But years later, in a conversation with *The Arizona Republic*, Jenni did not see it that way. "I feel more Mexican than American. Yes, I was born in the U.S., but that was just the place I was imported to."

None of this was of even the remotest concern to a child but, years later, in a conversation with the *Long Beach Press Telegram*, she acknowledged that she grew up straddling two cultures but had wholeheartedly embraced her Mexican roots. However she also offered that, even as a child, she was very much empowered in a way by being an American-born citizen.

"I learned to face the world," she reflected. "I learned that I wanted more for myself and that I wanted to become something."

CHAPTER THREE

SPANISH, *SÍ*; ENGLISH, *NO*

But first Jenni would have to grow up in a very traditional, very male-oriented Mexican environment. And that would not always be easy.

Don Pedro and Rosa ran a loving, family-oriented house. Her father was off to work each morning while her mother was the traditional homemaker. Money was tight and getting through the day was often a struggle but the children wanted for nothing. But as Jenni's first years played out, it was subconsciously apparent that she would have to function in a male-dominated world.

"I wasn't allowed to have dolls," Jenni told the *Dallas Morning News*. "My mom bought them for me but my brothers would tear them up and throw them away. They wanted to teach me karate, baseball, shooting marbles, and being a great wrestler. It made me tough. I got in trouble if I got into a fight and came home crying."

And when it came to music, the Rivera family functioned under an ironclad edict laid down by her *norteño*-obsessed father. "Growing up, my father did not allow us to listen to English music at home," she told *Billboard*. "*Norteño* was the first music that I listened to. But not just *norteño*. We would listen to mariachi. That's all I had. I had no choice."

However, being force-fed a steady diet of traditional Mexican music did have an up side: Jenni was introduced to and came to appreciate the likes of legends Lola Beltrán, Pedro Infante, and Ramón Ayala. "It's what my ears and heart was accustomed to hearing," she told *The Willits News*. "Classic Mexican music."

Jenni told the *Arizona Republic* that the Spanish-only rule did not stop at music. "We had to speak Spanish at home and could only listen to Spanish television. My father wanted us to remain and feel completely Mexican."

Don Pedro would later recall in an interview with *Hogar al Día* that he had a good reason for his Spanish-only rule. "In the beginning, my children did not speak English and I had to fight a lot to get them into school. At that time I felt a lot of anger filling me and so I told my children that, 'From this day onward, none of you are going to mention a word of English in the house. You can learn English outside but Spanish is going to dominate.'"

Her father's Mexican-music-only edict also only worked in the home. Once Jenni entered school, she quickly became enamored of American soul and pop music and would develop a particular attraction to the popular girl groups of the '60s. Mary Wells and The Supremes were her favorites. She loved the images, the music, the vibe of the times. Although she had missed the '60s, this kind of music had maintained a stronghold in the Mexican American community with such radio personalities as Art LeBeau and Huggy Boy continuing to fuel the interest in the oldies-but-goodies of the previous decade.

As it turned out, Don Pedro's insistence on Spanish music in the Rivera household may well have had more to do with his own dreams of being a music superstar than any adherence to his roots. Although he never spoke publicly of his own musical aspirations in the early days, the consensus was most certainly that along the way there had been an opportunity missed. Whatever the reality is, one thing is certain.

When it came to his children, he had the makings of a stage father.

He took every opportunity to attend shows and would often bring his children along . Jenni recalled in a *Billboard* conversation about the day her father took her to a show at the famed Million Dollar Theater in downtown Los Angeles, where legendary ranchero performer Vicente Fernández was holding court. Nobody could have been prouder than Don Pedro when, at one point in the performance, Fernández took the then four-year-old Jenni in his arms and did a walk around the stage.

Needless to say, once Don Pedro's children reached a certain age, their father was all over them, encouraging them to become performers in the *norteño*/mariachi tradition. He even went so far as to arrange singing lessons for Jenni and her two older brothers. Jenni was not thrilled.

"I never wanted to be a singer," she told *Open Your Eyes*. "My dad would take me to singing lessons when I was little. But I loved school. I thought education was important."

And that reflected in her early years in elementary school and, later, nearby Stevens Junior High School. Teachers would marvel at the young girl's interest and attentiveness in class. Her tests and school assignments were considered A level. At the time, low-income families and especially those who had emigrated from Mexico had a high failure and dropout rate. But Jenni was proving a glowing exception to the rule.

Although it was unspoken, the feeling was that Jenni's refusal to take music seriously caused a bit of tension between the young girl and her father. Also unspoken was her father's notion that by not wanting to sing roots music, she was somehow turning her back on her Mexican culture. It often resulted in vigorous arguments between Don Pedro and the much more practical Rosa.

Rosa saw the opportunities beyond music in America, knowing full well that a music career was often a land mine of alcohol, drugs, promiscuity, and careers that either never happened or were destroyed by the pressures of stardom and celebrity. She understood Don Pedro's fantasy of the music of their homeland but was often frustrated with his refusal to think beyond the past and look to the future.

"It was always a fight between my mom and my dad," Jenni recalled to *The Willits News*. "My dad wanted me to be a singer and my mom wanted me to have a traditional job like a nurse, teacher, or a doctor."

In the same interview, Jenni said that, as a youngster, she was on her mother's side. "I felt singing would be seen as the easy way out. So I never wanted to sing because I wanted people to see that I was intelligent enough to have a real career."

Finally at age eleven, Jenni, more to placate her father than out of any strong desire of her own, agreed to sing in public for the first time at Long Beach Hall. She was nervous as she waited off stage for her turn to perform. Her debut as a singer proved a total disaster. Jenni messed up the lyrics and, at mid-song, ran crying from the stage.

Waiting off stage was her father. He was beside himself with anger at his trembling daughter.

"My dad was mad at me," she told *OC Weekly*. "Not so much because I didn't win but because I chickened out."

Jenni would not sing again for another eleven years.

CHAPTER FOUR

PREGNANT PAUSE

But her father would.

In the early 1980s, a local East Los Angeles marketplace would often entertain lunchtime crowds with a band of musicians who would play traditional Mexican tunes. For a small fee, audience members who felt they had talent could step up and sing with the band. Don Pedro was hesitant but eventually took a chance, fronting the band. And both he and the audience discovered he was quite good in his renditions of traditional *norteño*, mariachi, and ranchera tunes. His presentation was heartfelt, sincere, and a bit world-weary; a momentary look back at the old days and ways for which many newly arrived Mexican immigrants were homesick. He would become a regular fixture at the lunchtime amateur performances and proved quite popular with his old-style tragedies, tales of struggles in their homeland.

Jenni was also going through changes.

She graduated from Stevens Junior high in 1982 with honors and matriculated to nearby Poly High School in Long Beach. By her sophomore year, she had become a shining star at Poly: friendly, outgoing, dedicated to learning, and a straight-A student. At fourteen years of age, the future looked bright with possibilities.

"I was one of the very few Mexican Americans who always made it to the honor roll," she said with pride to *The Willits News*. "I loved school and I always did my best. I felt I needed to have the determination and discipline to accomplish something for my family."

Reportedly Jenni also liked to party and was described in the *New York Daily News* as "a good time girl". But to what degree has never been revealed. If there was any acting out, it was most likely the normal challenges of being a teenage girl.

While far from being boy crazy, like any normal teenage girl, Jenni had begun to show interest in the opposite sex. And vice versa. One boy in particular stood out in Jenni's eyes.

José Trinidad Marín.

Little, if anything, has ever come to light regarding his background. He had piercing eyes, angular good looks, and, at a young age, was considered a catch among the fairer sex. How and where they met also is a mystery. What is known is that they began dating during Jenni's sophomore year at Poly High. They became intimate very quickly and, by the time Jenni had turned fifteen, she found herself pregnant.

While not thrilled with this situation, Jenni conceded to *Aquí y Ahora* that in the Mexican culture, this was just how things happened. "He was my husband because Mexican families...that's how they are. We had a relationship, I got pregnant, and then he was my husband."

But before that part of the cycle could take place, Jenni had to work up the courage to tell her parents that she was not only no longer a virgin, but that she was about to become a mother.

Jenni's parents did not take it well. According to a report in *The Huffington Post* referencing a 2002 interview, Jenni's parents were so upset that they kicked her out of the house. Jenni found herself in a situation sadly not uncommon in the low-income community.

"Usually, when a young girl is pregnant, she drops out of school and concentrates on being a mother," she explained to *OC Weekly*. "I thought that's what I had to do."

But she was saved from what could have bee been a dead-end life when her counselors at Long Beach Poly stepped in. They insisted she had too much promise to drop out and insisted that she enroll in Reid Continuation High School and graduate on time. Jenni was encouraged at the prospect of continuing her education. José was not.

Jenni elaborated on that tenuous situation with Marín in a far-reaching conversation with *Aquí y Ahora*. "I was the young, pregnant studious girl who wanted to keep studying. And he (José) was a macho Mexican man who told me I had to stay home, that I was going to be his wife, that I wasn't going to study and that was all done."

José Trinidad Marín was very much a "keep your woman barefoot and pregnant" kind of guy. He was openly hostile to the idea of Jenni continuing her education. By this time, they were married and living together and, according to an interview with Telemundo, "He wanted me to quit school and to stay home and cook and clean."

Jenni knew, even as she went through the process of carrying her first child to term, that the life José dictated she have was not the life she wanted.

The same year Jenni was going through motherhood and a new marriage, her father was taking the first steps toward realizing a lifelong dream.

In his travels, Don Pedro had come upon a box of discarded buttons that were going to be sold at the upcoming Summer Olympics in Los Angeles. He took the buttons and set up shop, selling the buttons on the streets of Los Angeles. Don Pedro was a quite persuasive seller and, even though the buttons were in less than ideal condition, they were selling quite easily to the tourists who had flocked to the city. By the time the Olympics were concluded, Don Pedro had earned $14,000, a tremendous amount for the Rivera family who always seemed to barely make ends meet. But Don Pedro had other ideas.

He wanted to take the money and put it into producing and releasing a record. His musical fantasies were now fueled by the even larger notion of producing his own records and becoming a mogul. His more practical wife, Rosa, was most certainly less than thrilled with the idea. But she was not about to step on his dream. With no recording experience and a shoestring budget, Don Pedro recorded his first album, a collection of mariachi music played by local musicians.

Jenni's father did not have a clue about record

companies and distribution deals. But he did know where Mexicans did a lot of shopping for goods, area swap meets. Occasionally Jenni and her brothers would go along and help their father out. Sadly, Don Pedro's record sold very few copies and did not recoup his investment.

In the meantime, the growing rancor between Jenni and José was temporarily put on hold in 1985 with the birth of Jenni's first child, a girl named Janney "Chiquis" Marín Rivera. The birth of her first child made Jenni all the more determined to provide a good life for herself and her daughter, so she began a clandestine journey in which she would constantly make excuses to José for her going out when, secretly, she was enrolled in Reid Continuation School. It was not easy, juggling the responsibilities of being a wife and mother while attempting to get her high school diploma. And Jenni recalled that when José did find out that Jenni was continuing her education behind his back, they fought. Often violently.

It was not uncommon that those fights would often end with José striking his wife. What was surprising was that Jenni, who knew better after being raised among many brothers and her father, would just as quickly hit him back. José would just as quickly back away when that happened. He knew it would not be good for his sense of machismo if the neighborhood found out that his wife was hitting him back and he was taking it.

With her marriage and the birth of their first grandchild, Jenni's parents' anger toward their daughter subsided and they were once more in her life, which was a positive because Rosa became a willing confidant in her daughter's continuing education. Her marriage to José was a whole other matter. A very dark side began to emerge after the birth of Janney. Jenni found José was a shortsighted, impatient man who was consumed by his own insecurities and quick to explode. When José raged at Jenni, verbal and physical abuse was sure to follow. Any love she had for this man was beginning to seep away . Jenni was young, inexperienced, and, for the most part, directionless. So she would put up with José's wrath and concentrate on the two most important things in her life: her daughter and her education.

In 1987, Jenni reached an important milestone. She graduated from Reid Continuation High School with honors as the class valedictorian. For most in her family and circle of friends, Jenni's graduation was considered a major accomplishment.

But Jenni was not finished.

Jenni's mind had always turned in the direction of business and entrepreneurship. She had dreams of someday opening and operating her own business. And so, shortly after graduating from Reid, she announced to her family that she was going to college to major in business administration. Aided by no less than eight scholarships, Jenni enrolled in business administration courses at Long Beach City College.

This time she did not hide the fact from her husband, José. He did not take the news very well.

Those who watched the slow disintegration of the marriage felt that José's manhood was being threatened by his wife attempting to better herself. By contrast, when he did work, Jenni's husband seemed content with the lowest-paying jobs he could find on the streets.

Whatever the reason, the reign of terror continued. In a piece by CNN Jenni was quoted as saying that the marriage was "absolute hell." She acknowledged that the physical and emotional abuse continued. But Jenni would continue to find solace in two different worlds: motherhood and education. In the former, she was loving, protective, and did her best to shield her daughter from the conflicts that would often erupt between José and her. Of the latter, higher education was a marvel. Learning from serious and encouraging people on a daily basis touched squarely on her innate desire to succeed and do better and it showed in excellent grades and a total understanding of the brave new world that education offered.

Jenni was not the only one seeking new challenges.

The same year she entered Long Beach City College, her father Don Pedro, despite the failure of his first release, decided to start his own record label out of a Long Beach storefront. Cintas Acuario Records was formed with the idea of releasing classic Mexican *corridos*. Don Pedro felt so well versed in the music that he was confident that he could in fact write and sing his own songs, and with a record label started on a shoestring, it would cut down on expenses. And so when Jenni gave him a pen for his birthday that year, he sat down and penned his first song, "La caída de Noriega" ("The Fall of Noriega") about Panamanian dictator Manuel Noriega. The song would be a reasonable independent hit upon its release, selling seven thousand copies in two weeks. Don Pedro could sense he was on the right track.

As was Jenni, who finished up a two-year degree at Long Beach City College and transferred to Long Beach State to fine-tune her business education. She was quite confident in her decision during a conversation with *Billboard*. "I was a straight-A student, I went to college, and I loved business."

Sadly, her home life was becoming an ever-increasing burden. She was falling into dark depression and, according to an article in *The Huffington Post*, she attempted suicide twice. But these truly dark days were more than balanced out by her responsibility toward her children and a growing determination to move forward.

She would concede in a *Qué Más* interview just how difficult her life had become. "Getting pregnant at age 15, juggling school with parenting and being in a domestic abuse situation. It was not easy."

Midway through her stint at Long Beach State, Jenni discovered she was once again pregnant. She was even-handed in her assessment of the situation. Her feelings about her husband at that point in the marriage were still not the best. But there was never any doubt she would have this baby. The intervening months would make Jenni's life even more strenuous as Jenni pursued higher education while chasing a toddler around and carrying another child in her womb.

Jacqueline Marín Rivera was born in 1989. Things just became more complicated. But it was nothing that Jenni could not handle. Jenni continued her education. José would continue to berate her and abuse her. But Jenni would often remark that she had learned a lot about growing up in a family of boys and so, by degrees, she would continue to fight back. She would present herself as a confident and educated woman in the face of José's blind hate and, more often than not, he would back down.

The couple continued to live right at the poverty line. There was money to make the rent but more often than not it was late. Food was the basics. Luxuries of any kind were nonexistent. They were living in a garage at one point. They had no car and Jenni's sole form of transportation was a bicycle. When the distance was not too great, she would walk. Buses were usually out of the question.

The rocky relationship continued and as she closed in on her business degree at Long Beach State in 1990, she once again found herself pregnant. As she struggled with the final days of college and the impending birth of a third child, Jenni was thinking deep thoughts about where her life was going.

And whether José would be part of it.

Jenni graduated from Long Beach State in 1991. Once she got beyond the excitement and praise for her accomplishment, she set about deciding what to do next. One thing was certain.

In 1992, she filed for divorce from José . José did not fight it. Like Jenni, he most likely had had enough as well. Her future was uncertain. She had a degree. She had no money and she had no job prospects. But one thing was certain. On her own with three small children to support, Jenni was not going to go into an emotional shell.

"Staying defeated, crying, and suffering was not an option," she told CNN. "I had to get off my feet, dust myself off, and press on."

CHAPTER FIVE

FOLLOW THE MONEY

Jenni was now free.

But the sense of relief that came from parting ways with José was short lived. José reportedly did not contribute any money to Jenni and his children post-divorce and so the reality was that the now single mother of three children was destitute. Jenni was forced to go on welfare.

Welfare was not an easy pill to swallow for Jenni. In her heart she was too self-reliant and forward-thinking to fall into that trap. But all the pride in the world was not going to keep her kids fed and a roof over their heads and so she reluctantly became another statistic on the welfare rolls of Southern California.

But it only took a few months before Jenni, driven to get out of the cycle of poverty she was falling into, put her business degree to good use when she landed a part-time job as a real estate agent with Century 21. It soon became evident that with her bubbling no-nonsense personality and drive to succeed, she was a natural in the real estate game and one who quickly began to rack up the sales in the competitive Southern

California real estate market. Ever the realist, Jenni would tell anybody who would listen that she got into real estate because that's where the money was. Things were starting to look up for Jenni. "I guess you could say that I was pretty successful," she told *Open Your Eyes*.

As was her father.

In 1992, Don Pedro wrote and recorded a modern-day *corrido*, "Corrido de los Disturbios" ('Ballad of the Disturbances') to tell the story of the Los Angeles riots that resulted from the beating of Rodney King. Nobody was more amazed than Don Pedro when the song sold 200,000 copies in two weeks . It was the boost Don Pedro's label needed. He began signing and recording more and more singers. He would follow with a series of anthology cassettes that capitalized on a thriving, albeit niche market of Mexicans interested in hearing stories about their anti-heroes' exploits in the world of drugs, crime, guns, and flashy cars. Cintas Acuario was suddenly a major player in the world of *narcocorrido* music.

In researching his book, author Elijah Wald had a front-row seat for the daily operation of Cintas Acuario and what he told this author was that the label was very much a family affair. "All the Riveras were kind of in the business," he recalled. "It was very much a family business. The Riveras, as a whole, impressed me in just how hard they worked at it. They were grabbing this small piece of the business."

While across town, Jenni was finding out what it meant to be truly on her own. When she was not with her children, she was working. Any kind of social life was the last thing on her mind. Becoming pregnant at fifteen had not allowed her to go through most of the teenage coming-of-age experiences. On a certain level, she was sad for having missed it. But she was far too focused on making a living and being a good mother to even consider such notions.

Until a few months into 1993 when, only a few months after her divorce was finalized, some friends rang her up and insisted she needed a night out with the girls. Their destination that night was the El Rancho Grande in Carson, California.

Jenni had claimed she had never had a shot of tequila in her life. Jenni drank a lot of tequila that night.

So much that when her girlfriends dared her to get on stage and sing, she drunkenly accepted the challenge. Her choice of song as she good-naturedly stumbled onto the stage was an old chestnut, "Las nieves de enero" (The Snows of January) by the late Chalino Sánchez who ironically had recorded several albums for Jenni's father. Jenni would recall in *Billboard* that the song went down well with the club's patrons.

"After I was done, all the other drunken people applauded me. I liked it."

Jenni's curiosity about singing and the entertainment world had been shaken. Her father had been thrilled when he found out about her drunken live performance, offering fatherly encouragement that she give it another try, this time sober. Her mother, not so much. For her part, Jenni was still not ready to take what many considered the next logical step. Her mind was on the business world. She had no desire to be a singing star.

However, she did like the idea of making money, so when her father's label had begun to become too big, Don Pedro asked his daughter to come and help him out. She agreed but the unwritten rule, and one that would continue to offer an undercurrent of tension, was that Jenni would not sing.

"I never thought of being a singer," she recalled in her final press conference in Monterrey, Mexico. "I never thought of all the artistic things that would happen in my career would happen. It wasn't my plan. It wasn't my dream or desire."

For the next year, Jenni would be a fixture in the Cintas Acquario office. Not surprisingly, she was competent in all matters involved in running a record label. On any given day she could be found performing the duties of sales rep, receptionist, publicist, office manager, and CD packager.

Wald recalled in a 2012 interview a typical day in the Cintas Acquario offices. Jenni was on the phone, talking to a "coyote" (a smuggler of Mexican illegals into America) and negotiating a price increase for a new label employee who was about to be brought across the border. All the while, her daughter Janney was racing around the office.

"Jenni was on the phone," reflected Wald. "She was perky, she was smart. She had the drive. It would not have surprised me if she had gone on to take over the office."

Jenni's older brother, Lupillo, had long ago been "chosen" by his father to become a singer of *narcorridos*, a hugely popular and, yes, controversial form of music that largely glorified the exploits of drug traffickers and those on the wrong side of the law.

With her brother now considered the star of the family, Jenni was relieved of the pressures from her father to also sing. But by watching the progress her brother was making, there was perhaps a spark of jealousy just below the surface.

With easy access to both musicians and a recording studio because of her father's label, Jenni decided to take a cautious first step by recording some songs to present to her father for an upcoming birthday present. The day-to-day operations at the label had brought her in regular contact with the Long Beach recording studio, as well as the musicians who were in and out on a regular basis. As office manager, it was not too difficult to arrange studio time when her father was not around. She wanted this special recording to be a surprise.

Especially if the reality turned out to be that she was not a very talented singer.

Jenni was most certainly excited and nervous recording for the very first time. She had chosen a safe first step; recording a series of *corrido* standards that included "Cruz de madera'" (Wooden Cross) and "Mi gusto es" (My Taste Is). Listening to those songs today, one can marvel at the passion and the sultry strength in Jenni's vocals. What she was drawing on during that first session was anybody's guess. But it was not hard to imagine that the trials and tribulations of her early life and abusive marriage factored into the emotion she brought to these songs. She would later admit that any early ventures on the music side, aside from currying favor with her father, were more of a hobby than anything else and that she had no intention of taking her music career any further.

Don Pedro was touched and impressed when Jenni presented him with the songs. But he was pleasantly surprised and shocked at the one original song that Jenni had written and recorded.

"La Chacalosa" (The Jackal Woman).

Casual listeners initially thought the song a decent novelty item; the idea of a woman singing *narcorridos*. But a closer listen quickly showed how groundbreaking the song was. The typical banda instrumental backing, big and boisterous, was countered by a lyrical twist in which the song's centerpiece was the daughter of a notorious drug trafficker who had learned from the best and was now out in the world of crime living by her own rules.

Lyrically it was a truly creative effort but Jenni has often admitted she was thinking more with her business mind than her creative side when she penned the song. "I figured if I was the only female who is going to sing one, then it's going to attract a lot of attention."

However there was more to "La Chacalosa" than dollars and cents. In a conversation with author Elijah Wald, Jenni talked about being different and getting attention.

"All the men were doing it and girls are bad girls, too. Not only do they like to listen to the music but there are women drug dealers. If you sing nice ballads like Mariah Carey and Celine Dion, you're just another artist. But if you sing about how you are a drug dealer and you can kill someone if he'll mess with you, then people are like 'Oh, she's very different.'"

Whatever her reasoning for creating "La Chacalosa", Don Pedro got the message. After hearing the song several times through, he reportedly smiled and said that he knew that one day she would do something in music. The divide between Don Pedro and Jenni was now officially closed.

Don Pedro was so impressed that he immediately pressed copies of his daughter's songs and put them out for sale. As Cintas Acurario was still a fairly Spartan operation, whose customers were primarily low-income Mexicans, Don Pedro literally ended up taking Jenni's first music to the streets, hawking his CDs at local area swap meets and flea markets. It was not uncommon to see Jenni at these outlets, smiling broadly, occasionally signing copies and engaging people as they passed by her booth. It was her first true brush with meeting the public as a performer.

That first album would be an introduction and nothing more. Jenni was not taking it all too seriously. That she was a local swap meet celebrity was good enough for her. It is safe to say the album did not sell a lot of copies.

Encouraged by the response, and perhaps to continue to cement the often estranged ties with her father, Jenni continued to write more songs. Her next big step in the evolution of her style would be an even more clearly defined blow for women's rights, "Las Malandrinas" (The Bad Girls). The song was a provocative, non-apologetic call to arms about women who came from the wrong side of the tracks and held up the hard drinking, hard clubbing, and overtly flirtatious ways as a badge of honor.

Given her natural feeling for *narcocorrido* and big and brassy *norteños* , it was surprising that the first few albums Jenni did for her father's label, most notably "Somos Rivera" (We Are Rivera) and "Con Los Viajeros Del Norte," (With Los Viajeros Del Norte) were fairly tame and nondescript, highlighted by good but undeveloped vocals.

"She had done a couple of albums," recalled Wald, "where she was just trying to be Celine Dion and it just wasn't happening."

With rare exception, Jenni was not showing an inclination to write her own songs and so, in a pattern that would present itself in all future efforts, these albums consisted primarily of already established, traditional *corridos*, rancheras, and mariachi tunes with the occasional original composed by an outside writer, usually tied in some way to her father's label.

Word spread locally about Jenni's music and while the albums were never more than a very local hit, they brought ever-increasing requests for Jenni to perform. Jenni continued to be reluctant about performing live. However the reality of having three mouths to feed, as well as the often up-and-down nature of the real estate business, ultimately won out.

"When I started getting calls (to perform) at local events and nightclubs, I would leave the kids with a babysitter and go out and make $100," she told *Billboard.* "All I wanted to do was to bring cheese, tortillas, beans, and whatever else I could get for the refrigerator."

But there were predators in the local club scene. Jenni came across one the night she agreed to do a show for a local club promoter for $300. After she finished her show, she was told by the promoter that he would only pay her if she slept with him. Jenni was so upset that she promptly decided to give up music altogether. Don Pedro recalled in a *Billboard* interview what happened next.

"I said to her, 'It's okay if you quit but please do me a favor first.' And that was when I asked her to do a *corrido* album."

Jenni thought about it for a while and agreed that someday she would.

Those privy to Jenni's earliest performances were often quick to dismiss the singer as a novelty act and with good reason. Jenni would reportedly dress big and bawdy in a sensual, revealing, and sometimes comedic way, looking like a larger-than-life version of a character in a Sergio Leone Italian western movie. But one thing even her detractors had to concede.

Jenni Rivera could most certainly sing.

CHAPTER SIX

EMOTIONS RULE

1995 would be a pivotal year in Jenni's life.

Although she had not completely given up on a career in the business world, her real estate work was gradually being eclipsed by a growing interest in the possibility of stardom as a singer. Her father had developed a strong business attitude as well, especially when it came to licensing his artists and their music to interested major labels. His fatherly pride very much in evidence, Don Pedro felt it was time that his daughter take the next step . Early in the year he had made Jenni's music a top concern and was fielding offers from some interested record companies.

"Before Jenni, it was all about Pedro and the way the business worked," Wald said of the way Cintas Acquario licensed their artists to bigger labels. "They had figured out in the big world they could do better licensing their stuff to major labels rather than having to deal with their own distribution."

Capitol/EMI's Latin division knew of Cintas Acquario's reputation in the Los Angeles area and assumed any album recorded on the cheap would do well in the already burgeoning Latin music market. Plus, they most likely reasoned, a good-looking woman on a CD cover was almost guaranteed to sell. The company agreed to a deal late in 1994 and before she knew it, Jenni was in the studio working on her first full-length album for a major label, "Chacalosa".

By this time Jenni was confident and comfortable in this musical environment and it showed in the freedom with which she was allowed to express her feelings of equality and empowerment. The songs on this first album told the time-honored tales of struggle, happy and not so happy endings, love lost and found and lost again; all within a modern retelling of the classic banda, ranchera, and mariachi style for today's people of the streets. Jenni would contribute two songs to the album that was rounded out by contributions from D.A.R., Wilfredo Elenes, Manuel Mauricio Guerrero, A.D. Jiménez, and Francisco Quintero. Jenni's developing style, big and brave vocals with sultry/innocent stylings and emotions, was rounding into shape. It was an approach to singing she was comfortable with.

The album was released in April 1995 . It would ultimately go on to sell one million copies over the years and go to the top of the U.S. Top Latin Albums. But most importantly, Jenni had kept her promise to her father.

Despite this strong start with her first big label release, Jenni instinctively went to a worst-case scenario: What if the singing did not turn her into a star? Her business side kicked in and she was already thinking of starting her own makeup and cosmetics line.

Wald related that his impression of Jenni at the time "Chacalosa" hit was of somebody who had not quite made up her mind. "At that point, she was still sitting in the office, answering the phone. She had the drive but I wouldn't have said necessarily to be a singer. I don't think anybody honestly felt she would be as big as her brother Lupillo. My guess was, at that point, she was just trying to get a little piece of the *corrido* world."

Jenni's musical progress was still being measured in small steps. Her appearances were still largely low-profile gigs at local clubs and halls. The money was not great but it was enough to keep her interest. Personally, Jenni seemed to be coming out of her shell. She was occasionally out and about with her friends in social settings and, not unlike the characters portrayed in the song "Las Malandrinas", she could let her emotions rule.

Which is exactly what happened in 1995 when she looked across a crowded bar and found Juan López looking back.

Like her first husband, López has remained largely a mystery. What is known is that he was street smart and no stranger to the wrong side of the law. But that night Jenni's logic took a backseat to what was pent-up lust. They hit it off immediately and in every possible way. This was Jenni's first real step into the dating/sex/relationship pool as an adult. Jenni most certainly was not looking for another José. But she sensed that Juan, while essentially cut from the same cloth, was not José; his demeanor was more laid back and, by degrees, less tied to the traditional notion of machismo . Throwing caution to the wind, Jenni immediately moved in with Juan.

Their relationship would only last a matter of weeks before Juan was arrested on allegations of smuggling undocumented immigrants across the border for pay. Juan was found guilty and sentenced to six months in prison. This should have been a sign that Jenni's new man was a mistake. Surprisingly, Jenni refused to cut and run and vowed to be there when Juan was released. Sure enough, six months later Juan was released from prison and shortly thereafter they moved in together.

When not handling her children, work, and a budding love life, Jenni was hard at work, hustling her music to the local Spanish language radio stations in and around Los Angeles. Despite her growing local notoriety and the fact that she was presenting a professional-quality album produced by a well-known label, Jenni ran afoul of a male-dominated radio industry that not only showed her little respect but could be downright rude and disrespectful, she related in a *Billboard* conversation.

"One radio programmer in L.A, the meanest sonovabitch in the world, threw my CD in the trash, right in front of my face."

Jenni was persistent in the face of numerous roadblocks set up by the programmers. In fact, she was surprisingly patient, calmly proclaiming that one day she would prove the people who had disrespected her wrong. That time would be sooner than anybody thought, because the winds of change were beginning to blow. A new generation of Mexican Americans was coming of age.

Jenni's peers, the children of Mexican immigrants

who had grown up in America were now a generation of two worlds: equally at home with their parents' traditional Latino culture but also eagerly embracing the new world of rap, soul, pop, and aggressive offshoots of *narcocorridos*. This new group was off the streets and the wild and crazy life of big cars, hot women, and the gang life. And it was reflected in their musical choices.

Which was not lost on the music industry.

Labels that had long relied on traditional Mexican music geared toward an older generation were now slowly moving into the brave new world, signing younger and edgier acts that were very much of the streets and catering to a new generation that culturally had much more on their plate.

Radio stations, which were notorious for changing their formats at the drop of a hat, suddenly were retooling to meet the needs of this new breed of consumer. Stations were popping up that were extremely *narcorrido* and new music heavy. Whereas traditional, old-school Mexican performers were the mainstay on traditional Latin music stations, the new stations were boasting playlists comprised almost exclusively of young Mexican American performers like Jenni. Seemingly overnight, Jenni was everywhere on the radio dial. And she was more than willing to give more.

Because of the nature of her contract with Capitol/EMI, Jenni was allegedly only obligated to give the company one more album. The album, entitled "Farewell to Selena", also released in '95, was a full-blown dramatic and emotional tribute in song to the late legendary Tejano singer Selena. Before the year was out, Jenni would show how prolific she could be when she released "We Are Rivera" (Ayana Musical) and ''Con Los Viajeros del Norte'' (Kimos Music) before the end of 1995.

The latter two albums cut very close to her previous releases, a mixture of traditional forms coupled with subtle forays into an edgier but still commercially acceptable sound. Jenni was still following the money. She knew what her fans wanted and what the radio stations would play and she was more than happy to give everybody what they wanted.

Jenni's tribute to Selena proved to be much more than an easy cover album. No matter what anyone thought of the songs, nobody could argue with her growing sense of sincerity and conviction. While the songs on all three albums were all over the board in terms of pop and commercial sensibilities, they were all uniformly saved by the performer.

By the time the year ended, Jenni was in the best possible bliss. In the world of Spanish-language music, she was well on the way to being a star. She was living with a man with whom, despite some observers' reservations, she seemed genuinely in love. And of course there were her children. Always the children.

Things could not have been more perfect in her world when, in the early months of 1996, her sister Rosie dropped a bombshell.

She revealed a long-kept secret. Since 1987, when Rosie was 16, and since 1991 when Jenni's daughter Janney was 12, José had been sexually molesting them. Each knew about the other but agreed it would be best to keep this a secret from Jenni. And as Jenni recalled with *Aquí y Ahora*, with good reason.

"They had promised not to tell me anything because of my character," she painfully recalled. "They were afraid of what he (José) would do and that I would wind up in jail."

Janney would explain in preliminary testimony, chronicled by the *Long Beach Press Telegram*, that her father had threatened to send her to Mexico to live with his mother if he told anybody. She further stated that a fear of what her mother might do if she found out had kept her from talking.

"I was afraid my mom would get very angry. I felt that she would probably kill him or something and that she would be sent to jail and my father would be dead. I didn't know where I was going to be. I was just afraid."

Jenni's sister, Rosie, was also silent out of fear but she related in pre-trial testimony covered by the *Long Beach Press Telegram*, Paparazzi TV and Escándalo TV and Guidelive.com, that seeing her family's reaction to a similar case gave her the courage to come forward.

"There was a story about another girl being molested by an adult and I remember one of my brothers defending the girl and believing her immediately. So I said, 'If they believe her, then they'll for sure believe me and they'll defend me and protect me.'"

Not unexpectedly, Jenni was irate when she was finally told. But she felt even more guilty because, at the time the molestation of Janney began, she had not yet begun singing and was around her daughter all the time—except when she was sleeping. Her husband had assaulted his daughter mere feet from where she lay.

Once her emotions were in check, Jenni moved swiftly, filing sexual assault charges against José and a warrant was immediately put out for his arrest. Word traveled swiftly along the street telegraph that was Long Beach and José became quickly aware e was about to be arrested.

José vanished without a trace.

CHAPTER SEVEN

QUIET TIMES

Going into 1997, Jenni was a woman of many minds.

She was an ongoing presence in the halls of law enforcement, constantly checking on how the police were progressing in tracking down José. She had her little ones to take care off and a new life with Juan.

But her music was never far from her thoughts. With her previous albums she had proven a distinctive voice in all manner of Mexican music genres. Many early critics had attempted to typecast her as a specific type, largely based on the success of her early albums as a female *narcocorrido* singer. It was an easy tag given her two early *narcocoriddo*-style hits, despite the fact that the vast majority of her songs to date had been in the traditional banda, ranchera, and mariachi mold. But Jenni was having none of the typecasting and would often point to an individual style as her stock in trade.

"My music has always been 'Jenni'," she said in an Univision conversation. "I always come up with the concepts for my albums. I've always known what I have wanted to say in my music."

Jenni was, for all intents and purposes, on a break between 1997 and 1999 but would occasionally go into the studio and do an album that would be released through her father's label or one of its distribution outlets.

And what Jenni wanted to say on the January 1997 release, "Jenni" (Balboa Music Corporation) was a lot. Her voice ranged far and wide on a series of banda tunes; alternately raucous and sultry, Jenni showed that, less than a half dozen albums into her career, she was already near the top of the best the distaff side of Mexican music had to offer.

Many observers of Jenni's career have claimed that "Jenni" was her true breakout album. Her vocal stance was, by this time, fully formed. The production values had risen to a high polish. And the reality was that Jenni had experienced much personally and had, with this album, struck an emotional balance between personal and creative in her music.

But all accolades aside, the frustration of being a big fish in a small and often neglected pond was beginning to get to the singer. There were many labels that were quite good at marketing traditional Mexican music but did not understand the complexity of the new music movement being spearheaded by, among others, Jenni. So despite the fact that her records were critical raves, the level of sales was slow in coming.

For a while Jenni considered taking her next album to Sony, where her brother, Lupillo, recorded. But she felt confined and not really appreciated as an individual under the umbrella of the mega corporation. And although she never said so publicly, the consensus was that she chaffed at being regulated to "Lupillo's little sister". So she held back on an album that was already near completion and just decided to bide her time. Just as well—

Because suddenly there was a far more pressing issue to deal with.

She was also about to become a mother for the fourth time. Jenni had always made no bones about the fact that she loved children and would like a lot of them. She was also quite insistent that she and Juan would have to be married. Juan agreed. Culture and expectation once again were rewarded and Juan and Jenni were soon married.

Jenni's fourth child, Jenicka López Rivera, was born that same year.

To the world at large, Jenni seemed to step away from the spotlight over the next year, caring for her growing family and contemplating her next move; living in relative anonymity in the city of Compton. But with those whose hands were on the pulse of the Los Angeles music movement, the reality was that Jenni was putting out music, only on a much smaller scale. With no major label interest on the horizon, Jenni returned to her roots and recorded a pair of albums for her father's Cintas Acuario label (and subsequently licensed to Sony Music), "Si quieres verme llorar" (If You Want to See Me Cry) and "Reyna de reynas" (Queen of Queens), her first two full-length studio albums, which were released in 1999.

With the release of the two albums, Jenni reverted to business/hustle mode. She was constantly on the new wave of Spanish-language radio stations, offering up interviews and gossipy news tidbits and all the while imploring programmers to just give her albums a listen. Eventually the local stations gave in, and several cuts off the "Reyna de reynas" began getting airplay on the suddenly influencial station Radio Qué Buena.

Both albums were an enticing mixture of styles and indicated that while Jenni had *narcocorrido* in her soul, she was more than capable of showing her talents in variations on ranchero, Tejano, and mariachi. Love songs and ballads were not beneath her and she showcased a soulful take on tried-and-true romantic notions.

Predictably, both albums did quite well in the Los Angeles area and in pockets nationally and in Mexico, as the all-important radio play was beginning to swing her way. Things were starting to change. The trickle of radio interest that had marked the previous upswing was now in full motion. Late into '98 and into '99, the radio scene had become younger and hipper. Young people were calling in, requesting the hip new sound and, in particular, Jenni's songs.

"Si quieres verme llorar" sold 12,000 copies during its first week of release and would go to number one on the Top U.S. Latin Album Charts. "Reyna de reynas" would do equally well; it debuted at number five on the Top U.S. Latin Album Charts and, within three weeks, would sit at number one.

With her records doing well, Jenni began to think about getting out and playing live on a more regular basis. A household of children and a new husband had always been a good excuse not to. But with increased demand to see her live, Jenni sensed it was time to hit the stage.

Jenni live was a three-ring circus of sight and sound.

Alternately cursing and drinking between songs, Jenni was a dreadlocked, larger-than-life presence, constantly in control of her voice and her songs, playing both lyrical and emotional lead and backup to her band. To a large degree, Jenni's live performance was still considered a novelty act, a cartoonish feminine counter to the manly world of *narcocoriddo*. But things had started to change in the live performances. Jenni had evolved beyond mere eye candy for the men and curiosity for the ladies. The whoops and hollers that greeted Jenni live were no longer derisive but full of support, enthusiasm, and no small amount of wonder.

But the atmosphere in the crowded, smoky clubs definitely shot up when Jenni would inevitably turn on her *narcocorrido* alter ego for her signature "hardcore" songs, "La Chacalosa" and "Las Malandrinas." The crowd went spectacularly wild but the keen observer could see it in the eyes, the screams, and the suddenly defiant stance . Women found empowerment for women in those songs. Suddenly for Latinas, there was revolution in the air.

"My concerts are very emotional, they're real," she offered in her final press conference. "There's a lot of celebrating. A lot of fun. That experience includes all that it means to be an artist and a woman."

It translated into Jenni's profile rising in the eyes of major labels. Fonovisa/Universal would be a particularly enticing suitor. Nearly all of their artists were Mexican so they knew their way around what was perceived as 'niche marketing.' The company made it plain that Jenni would not just be one of the herd when it came to publicity and marketing. She was wined and dined with promises of being very big.

And that's exactly what Jenni wanted.

CHAPTER EIGHT

CAUTION: HITS AHEAD

Signing on with Fonovisa/Universal was cause for celebration in the Rivera household and in the halls of Cintas Acuario. The family was excited at the prospect that there would be no half stepping when it came to the all important elements of marketing and distribution of Jenni's music. They also sensed that it was of equal importance that the singer's first album for Fonovisa, likewise, had to be pure Jenni with no compromises.

While she had made some 'new' waves with her song 'La Chacolasa' and her outrageous local shows in Los Angeles, the reality was that much of her recorded output to that point had fairly traditional ranchera and Tejano ballads.

This time things would be different and very much a family affair.

Cintas Acuario, essentially Pedro, would be heading up all production elements of Jenni's new album, 'Que me entierren con la banda' (May They Bury Me With The Banda). Although there would be a handful of outside writing contributions, most of the credits would read either Cintas Acuario, Jenni Rivera, or in one instance, a resurrection of an old Pedro Rivera chestnut 'Sinaloa Princess Norteño'. The album's title track featured a duet between Jenni and her brother Lupillo.

Jenni's growing skills as a songwriter would also be on display with the songs 'Que un rayo te la parta' (May A Ray Take it Away), 'Solo se da amor' (It Only Gives Love) and an early writing effort now dusted off and reborn, the very much narcocorrido oriented 'Las Malandrinas'.

Jenni was proceeding cautiously. Nobody was certain how an upfront female was going to come across on the national stage and so the involvement of Jenni's father and brother may well have been an attempt to soften her entry into the big time. Nobody is really sure how Jenni reacted to her family being very much a part of her business. But apparently all egos were in check and father and brother most certainly offered minor recording suggestions but then just sat back and let Jenni be Jenni.

'Que me entierren con la banda' was released on March 27, 2000. Almost instantly 'Las Malandrinas' became a runaway hit. The song was an across-the-board addition to Spanish-language radio playlists. Listeners were constantly calling stations to request the song. And just like that, Jenni was suddenly a star.

That song had struck a nerve. Latin women had an anthem that was their flag carried high on the march to equality. Ever the businesswoman, Jenni took a pragmatic approach to the song's instant success, citing an untapped market for her music in the female audience. "I wrote it as an homage to my female fans," she told *Billboard.* "The type of girls who go clubbing, drink tequila, and stand up for themselves."

Jenni also acknowledged in an *OC Weekly* interview that "Las Malandrinas" was also her way of distancing herself from the cliche female Mexican pretty bodies who sang soft ballads. "I wanted to convey a message that women could be as bad-ass as men. Mexican society is going to be macho forever. But with so many people moving to the United States, it's changing. Mexican women can no longer sit there expecting men to support them. Either you get off your ass and make something of yourself or you starve."

The album would end up at number one on U.S./Latin, Mexico and Italy sales charts. The reviews were overwhelmingly positive. Sadly, when the album topped out at a mere half million copies sold worldwide, it would be Jenni's poorest-selling album to date.

The result of this album and the impact of the hit led to Jenni's first brushes with touring outside the Los Angeles area and in states where large Mexican populations proved equally accepting of Jenni. Those early national dates were an exciting time for Jenni. No longer a local Los Angeles act, Jenni was seeing her impact expanding and, to her way of thinking, assuring a long career.

With the chart success of "Que me entierren con la banda", Jenni found that the perks of celebrity could be a double-edged sword. She was an outgoing personality who dealt easily with most of the early brushes with adulation. But living a low-key home life soon began to suffer. Enterprising fans soon figured out where Jenni lived and would regularly stop by her home, often in the middle of the night, to simply stand outside her house and stare. It was not uncommon for Jenni to be puttering around the house in her pajamas and hear a knock on the door, where an excited fan would be standing and asking for a photograph. Initially the intrusions were understandable. Jenni's large reputation was of a bad-ass so it was not unreasonable to associate her with living in a rough part of town.

But Jenni needed her sleep, because midway through 2000, she discovered she was once again pregnant. Jenni was happy at the news but it was becoming evident that children and a career that was suddenly taking off was a lot to deal with twenty-four/seven. The gregarious woman who made no bones about craving the spotlight suddenly just wanted some peace and quiet.

She was not going to get it in Compton. By 2001, Jenni and her family had moved to Corona, California.

Jenni was nothing if not prolific and, as a businesswoman, was not going to let the success of her first Fonovisa album run its course without having a follow up album waiting in the wings. Or, as it would turn out, two albums. "Se las voy a dar a otro" (I'm Giving Them To Another) and "Déjate amar" (Let Yourself Love) were put together as logical follow-ups; a platter of different styles, playful remakes of the Freddy Fender classic "Wasted Days and Wasted Nights" and Rosie And The Originals' "Angel Baby." Jenni's tunes, as well as those from outside composers, mixed and matched easily and in a crisp manner.

Observers of Jenni's musical evolution tend to look at these two albums as fairly minor efforts. But the reality is that on these albums, and on such songs as "Mi vida loca" (My Crazy Life), "Chicana Jalisciense" (Jalisco Chicana) and "El nopal" (The Prickly Pear), Jenni was in the middle of a very important watershed moment. Both albums were very roots-oriented, painting a reverent and vibrant picture of the *norteño*/ranchera form. However, it was also evident that throughout the albums, Jenni was reaching into the future—embracing modern elements while paying homage to the past.

If there was a giant step forward, it was in Jenni's embracing of studio technology. On previous albums it was essentially Jenni singing and the band playing with simple overlaps. To the practiced ear, there was nothing dynamic about the production values. However, beginning with her 2001 albums, Jenni began to play around with studio tricks, occasional echo, the playing up of certain vocal and instrumental moments for dramatic effect. "Se las voy a dar a otro" and "Déjate amar" were a step forward in Jenni's growing comfort in the studio.

While both albums sold extremely well, it remained for the song "Querida socia" (Dearest Girlfriend) off "Déjate amar" to cement Jenni's skyrocketing reputation. But in the eyes of many, she was still a one-hit wonder. Jenni recalled in *Billboard* the importance of that second hit single. "I started getting more offers to perform across the U.S. It was a sign that I could do this a bit longer."

Around that time, Jenni made the acquaintance of Flavio Morales, presently the senior vice president of programming and production for Mun2. Morales had been a local producer at the time and had been working with Jenni's brother, Lupillo. Through Lupillo, Morales got to know Jenni and would remember in *The Hollywood Reporter* that he was impressed with her style, her "cool" and that she was equally conversant in 2Pac as she was in traditional Mexican music. His instincts told him Jenni had potential. Possibly in the world of reality television.

"We met in a restaurant and spoke for a couple of hours," he recalled. "But reality television was not something she wanted to do. She loved reality but didn't want to be one."

It was just as well because, with the birth of her fifth child, Johnny López Rivera in 2001, Jenni was back to being a mom and temporarily out of the spotlight. That was fine with her.

"Being a mother is by far my favorite and most important career," she insisted to The Associated Press. "They (her children) take priority over everything else."

Comments like this were not just "spin moves" to build a good public relations profile. Her family was serious business, as she insisted to Fox Latino News. "Everyone thinks my world revolves around my celebrity, my music career, or my successes. But it's not like that. My children need attention. It makes my role as a mother fulfilled."

While motherhood was number one on her agenda, her business and musical sense was never far behind . She had become more confident and mature and, by association, more independent from the influence of her family and, in particular, her father Don Pedro. A showdown of sorts between father and daughter seemed inevitable. But rather than a sudden break, Jenni and Don Pedro's split was low key and subtle.

"There was certainly a moment in the early 2000s where Jenni really split off (from her father) said author Wald in 2012. "She took over her own business and the impression was that she said, 'I'm headed out on my own'. She got her own people and all of a sudden she could not be reached at her father's label."

The split appeared to be without rancor, although one can speculate that the father/daughter relationship was most likely strained. But the family was always welcome to Jenni's show and they were nothing if not supportive which, according to Wald, was par for the course with the Rivera clan.

"They were competitive," he said. "But they were also very supportive of each other. I'm sure they were competitive when it came to things like whose record was selling more or things of that nature. I'm sure there were moments. But it certainly appeared that everybody was very helpful and supportive."

While out of sight, Jenni was definitely not out of mind when it came to honors. 2002 was her first brush with awards when, in September, she experienced the glitz and glamour of Hollywood as she walked down the red carpet for the Latin Grammy Awards at the famed Nokia Theater as a nominee for Best Banda Album Of The Year. She would not win that award but followed up the same year as Best Female Solo Singer at the Premios De La Radio presentation.

Jenni was on top of the world going into 2003. But the ride would not be smooth.

CHAPTER NINE

DRAMA

Jenni could sense something was going on.

Outwardly Juan López was the ideal husband. He did not exert any macho jealousy as he stood by and watched Jenni's career take off. He was good with the children. In the best possible way, he was not Jenni's first husband, José. There was only one problem.

Juan had been cheating on Jenni for quite some time.

It has never been fully explained how long the pattern of infidelity played out or to what degree Jenni did or did not know what was going on. What has been reported on Latino Fox News and other outlets was that the last straw was when Jenni walked in on her husband in bed with another woman. Jenni's response was quick and decisive. She immediately filed for divorce, which was finalized in 2003.

Feeling deceived by a man a second time did not sit well with Jenni. While her first husband had committed the more heinous crime, Juan's deception brought out pure anger in the singer.

"I found out that he was cheating and I was going through hell," she admitted to the *San Antonio*

Express. "Just being cheated on by the one you love can destroy you if you let it. He was out there getting all the girls and stuff and I was working hard, being a real estate agent, a housewife, and a mother."

Jenni did her best to keep the divorce out of the press. To no avail.

"In 2003 we separated and there was a divorce that I thought wouldn't be made public," she told the interview program *Aquí y Ahora.* "But it became very public."

Jenni was faced with the sadness and embarrassment of her second marriage dissolving. She was angry, much in the way she had reacted with José. But unlike that first marriage, she would continue to have positive feelings about Juan and, in the ensuing years, she made sure her children got to know their father .

The stresses in Jenni's personal life only served to fuel her creative spirit. Rather than another album of new material or reworking traditional songs, Jenni now envisioned a concept album in which she looked to the great Mexican women who had already made their mark and had paved the way for her. Thus was born "Homenaje a las grandes" ("Homage to the Great Ones") in which she paid tribute to the music of legendary singers Lucha Villa, Mercedes Castro, Rocío Dúrcal, Lola Beltrán, Alejandra Guzmán, and, with one English language track, to Diana Ross with a cover of the song "Where Did Our Love Go".

Jenni recalled the labor of love that was "Homenaje a las grandes" in the *El Paso Times.* "I don't like to call myself a feminist. But I've supported feminine talent since I was a little girl. I loved to honor all the different songs and lyrics of these strong women."

There was a reverential tone in the studio during the recording of the album. While wanting to add that "Jenni" twist to the songs, Jenni was also careful to make sure the essence of what had made the singers and the songs classics was uppermost in her mind. And the Diana Ross cover? Well, the business side of Jenni was most likely hoping a couple of English-language stations would take the bait and play it, thus giving U.S. audiences their first taste of Jenni.

The album received across the board positive reviews, with critics citing how well organized and thoughtful the project was. But while a critics' favorite, positive reviews did not translate into a monster hit and the album stalled at number 37 on the U.S. Latin Album Charts.

Despite seemingly stalled on the album sales charts, nobody could doubt the quality and substance of her music, which was why she once again snagged nominations for the 2003 Latin Grammys for Top Female Performer and Best Album categories. But the reality was that Fonovisa was very much a bottom-line corporation and, inside the executive offices, the dollars-and-cents people were concerned that Jenni's albums had not produced financially.

One thing remained certain: Jenni's popularity as a live performer had grown to the point that, by 2003, she was beginning to move up the performing food chain from the small bars and clubs to bigger clubs and bigger paydays. Bigger halls and concert venues were still a way off but she was easily filling higher-end places.

Like El Rodeo Club in Los Angeles.

El Rodeo Club was a bit on the pricey side. The price of admission was $35. If you wanted a table, you had to buy a $100 bottle of tequila. The majority of their clientele were low-income people who often had to work three days just to make the price of admission. But when Jenni was performing, she would typically sell out the place, because the audience knew they would get their money's worth and one hell of a time.

Live Jenni circa 2003 was a literal force of nature. Equal parts theater and music, Jenni would earn constant points through her music and her actions that her, by now, largely female audience and her were a lot alike.

"People like to think that I am as normal as they are," she told Billboard. "It's (the show) is all to show how accessible I am. That I am just like you. Not better."

Wald agreed with Jenni's explanation. "She had an intense connection with her audience which was hugely Mexican women who did not look like movie stars. It was very much about the fact that they were as sexy and beautiful as all those skinny girls out there."

He also explained that the typical Jenni show of that period revolved around a specific set of themes: the funny girl and the tough girl, all of which was presented in a fun, family-oriented way.

A big part of her show's drive to be just like the audience was that, throughout the set, she would constantly accept shots of tequila from members of the audience and down them. Usually late in the show, somebody would hand her yet another shot. Jenni would then feign "no more, please" before dramatically taking the latest shot and downing it to wild applause. Jenni's drinking antics eventually led to media reports that the singer was an alcoholic.

Jenni made a point of good-naturedly defusing that rumor during a conversation with *Aquí y Ahora*. She said she did not drink at home or socially expect for what she termed "special occasions".

"I don't have a problem with alcohol," she continued. "We get on quite all right. Alcohol and I get on just fine. I don't exceed it or abuse it."

Jenni was not one to confine her live shows to the accommodating clubs of Los Angeles. As her reputation grew she would often make the trek to Mexican border towns like Ciudad Juárez to perform. These were dangerous times along the U.S./Mexican border. Drugs were a thriving business in the towns where Jenni went and by association, so was crime, violence, and sudden death. And Jenni would be candid in saying that every time she crossed the border to perform, she was scared to death. She had friends who had braved those rough towns who had been kidnapped or murdered and she was well aware that stepping on stage in those unstable places could be courting bad things. She would have security with her when she played across the border. But, as she explained to *Billboard*, all she could do is pray.

"I pray to God to give me grace and get me safely back home. There's really not much else I can do."

Ever the businesswoman, Jenni was already working hard in 2003 and into 2004 to establish her growing brand in areas other than music . The long-talked-about cosmetics line was now ready to go public, as was a beauty salon franchise that would be managed by her daughter Janney. Perhaps the perfect example of Jenni's business sense and generosity was her decision to open up her own real estate business with offices in Long Beach and Corona for the specific purpose of helping immigrants to buy their first home.

With all her growing business interests and the constant issues surrounding both her family and professional life, it was not surprising that Jenni was not in a frame of mind in 2003 to rush back into the studio and put together another album. According to reports, Fonovisa was getting impatient with a lack of new product and not too delicately insisted that Jenni record another album . Jenni dug in her heels. She would not be rushed. Finally Fonovisa threw up its hands and a compromise was reached.

Midway through 2004, a greatest-hits collection, "Simplemente...La mejor" (Simply...The Best) was released. Both sides knew what the record was: a stopgap measure to keep interest in Jenni high until she decided to record again. Granted, the album was a solid collection of Jenni's early hits and a tidy introduction to those who had come upon Jenni late. But neither Jenni or Fonovisa could have predicted the commercial and critical impact. "Simplemente...La mejor' would sell 14,000 copies its first week of release and would debut at number one on the U.S. Latin Album Charts. The album, which would ultimately go on to sell more than five million copies, was also the best reviewed album of Jenni's career to that point.

What was not reported until January 2013 in the *Huffington Post* and *People en Español* was that Jenni, sometime during 2004, also recorded a series of

'Americanized' songs especially suited for the English-language market. For whatever reason, Jenni had decided not to submit those tracks to her label and they were promptly put into a vault for safekeeping. The nature of those songs and whether or not they were truly up to Jenni's standards would be anybody's guess.

Jenni's growing reputation as an electrifying performer continued to grow well into 2005, so much so that she was now regularly headlining larger 5,000-seat venues such as the Kodak Theater and the Gibson Amphitheater. These larger venues seemed to demand a larger performance. Costume changes became an important element of the show. From a revealing leather outfit and ball cap when singing her tough girl songs to an all-white gown when singing romantic ballads, a Jenni show was now taking on more and more of a theatrical atmosphere.

There were also moments of sexually charged humor and set pieces. The scene that inevitably brought the house down was when Jenni called four male members of the audience to the stage, sat them in a row of chairs facing her and had her stage security guards pin their hands behind them. Then while singing an erotically charged song, she would give each of the men a lap dance. It was moments like this that catapulted the "Jenni Rivera Experience" from mere concert to all-out spectacle.

When not recording or performing, Jenni was in a highly reflective mood in 2005. And a lot of what she was thinking about put her in a dark mood. The failed marriages, the abuse, the struggles of a Latina trying to make it in the world. Now into her thirties, Jenni had experienced a lot, overcome a myriad of obstacles and stereotypes, and had emerged flawed but well on the way to being a star performer and an accomplished businesswoman. Jenni had a right to be satisfied with her life at that moment.

But what Jenni was feeling when she went into the studio to record "Parrandera, Rebelde y Atrevida" (Party Girl, Rebel and Daring) was frustrated, angry, and bitter. And what came out was quite possibly Jenni's best, most personal and emotionally wrought album.

To be sure, Jenni had been down the angry and bitter road in previous albums. But she was younger then. With this album Jenni discovered that being a woman of a certain age now infused her with a world weariness that made her real life-influenced songs all the more poignant and defiant. But albums this dark and personal don't usually find massive commercial success. However "Parrandera, Rebelde y Atrevida" was nothing if not on the side of radio friendly. Always a student of all the great ladies of song, despite the music style, Jenni seemed to have found a torchy "I Will Survive" vibe that made this album more than a series of personal rants.

It is why the album would spin off three solid singles, "De contrabando" (Of Contraband), "No vas a creer" (You Won't Believe), and "Qué me vas a dar" (What Are You Going to Give Me) onto the charts of several regional and national charts. The album would sell more than a respectable 9,000 copies on release and would debut at number one on the U.S. Latin Album Charts.

"The music came easy to me," she said of the

album in a conversation with *Billboard.* "It's in my blood. It's in my culture. I know these people. I know how they live. I know how they react."

Jenni was heartened by the success of the album, feeling fulfilled as both an artist and a woman . Her reputation was continuing to grow and the result was that she was playing bigger concert venues. But the reality was that even at this level, it was continuing to be a hard road.

From the beginning, Jenni had made no bones about the fact that she wanted to be a breakout artist who would cross over into the all-important English-language market. However, even with her best album to date making noise, she was still a Spanish-language singer. Her U.S. dates outside of her regular Los Angeles appearances were sporadic at best. English language radio stations would not touch her music and press coverage in the U.S. was scant.

Jenni remained determined to make it big in the country of her birth. "People don't know me," she told *Spanish Town.* "But they will."

It was this level of drive and competitiveness in Jenni that was typical of the entire Rivera clan. They were supportive of each other but the competitive juices lurked just below the surface. Although Jenni would often state publicly that she had no rivalry with her family members, the relationship between Lupillo and her had suddenly become strained. The reason was never made public, although ego and who was the most popular performer were most likely in the mix. What is known is that by 2005, Lupillo and Jenni were barely speaking and, for all intents and purposes, estranged.

CHAPTER TEN

AND THE LAW WON

José Trinidad Marín had been on the run since 1996, living the fugitive life of odd jobs, crash pads, and the constant fear of the police knocking on the door. But what José had not counted on was that he would eventually be brought to justice because of an unexpected source.

What nobody had counted on was the fanatically loyal fan base Jenni had gathered over the years. Not only were they interested in her stardom but her personal life as well. They knew everything there was to know about her marriage to José and the horrifying discovery of his sexual abuse. Jenni's fans took it upon themselves to help in the only way they could—which was to keep an eye out for José.

In April, 2006, a group of fans spotted José on the street in Riverside, California, and immediately called the authorities. José was taken into custody.

Jenni was overjoyed at the news but that joy was tempered by the fact that while justice would now finally be done, her celebrity would be all over the case and what many were already predicting would be a long, drawn-out, and very traumatic trial. What she would find out later in the year was that justice moved slowly and she was more than a bit concerned when, in October 2006, José was let out on bail while awaiting the trial. The singer was concerned her ex might once again flee and disappear. However, the authorities had a short leash on him and he was never a flight risk.

Still with all the recent news in her personal life, Jenni once again appeared distracted and unable to focus on what many considered would be the all-important follow-up to "Parrandera, Rebelde y Atrevida" . But rather than put pressure on Jenni, both the singer and Fonovisa had already created a Plan B for just such a situation. Over the past two years, Fonovisa had seen fit to record several of Jenni's live performances for later use. Jenni's would be the rare live albums that would not be considered mere filler to cover for songwriter's block. Her performances had become quite legendary for those who had caught her act. She had enough studio albums under her belt to justify such a disc. And it went without saying that a Jenni "live" CD was something people had been asking for.

Shortly after Jenni's ex-husband was taken into custody, "En vivo desde Hollywood" (Live From Hollywood), a live performance taped in Las Vegas, was released. Five months later, a second live album. "Besos y copas desde Hollywood" (Kisses and Cocktails from Hollywood), recorded at the famed Kodak Theater in Hollywood, was released. Both served as serviceable memories of Jenni's live show but were ultimately not super chart-toppers. And a big part of that might have been too much at once. Jenni's fans could justify buying one live album. But two so close together of essentially the same set? Not so much.

But those releases did give the singer some time to do some soul-searching and the result was that, early in 2007, she once again went into the studio to record "Mi vida loca" (My Crazy Life), a taut distillation of the ups and downs of her life. This was a daring experiment on a number of fronts. With twenty-seven songs, the album was easily the equivalent of two albums. The album contained spoken-word intros to many of the songs, giving insight and drama in a very personal way; self-examination through song, if you will. The album also contained two English-language songs, Gloria Gaynor's disco empowerment anthem "I Will Survive", and "Look At Me Now" . "Mi vida loca" was a soundtrack of her life and times.

Very biographical and very to the point, "Mi vida loca" was being touted as Jenni's further foray into putting down real life as a song. Observers of the Latin music scene were holding their breath as the days counted down to a June 2007 release. Would this album finally break out of the Latin world and at least take a small foothold beyond those confines or would it showcase Jenni as a performer comfortable in telling her tales while sticking closely to her Mexican roots and heritage?

Jenni offered that the genesis for "Mi vida loca"'s obvious autobiographic elements was an attempt to set the record straight. "My life has been so put out there by the media that I figured I might as well put it out there myself in my own words and through my music," she told *Billboard*. "I wanted (to use the album) to clear up speculation about my private life."

By the time the second live album was released, Jenni was already many months into monitoring her ex-husband's case as it made its way through the Long Beach, California, court system. The trial of José Trinidad Marín would ultimately last two years.

The preliminary hearings would last right up until the start of the trial on April 30. By that time emotions were raw. Jenni had been a regular spectator at the pre-trial hearings. It was difficult, as she explained to Guidelive.com, of Dallasnews.com.

"Now that he's arrested, it's hard to go back and relive everything and go to court when you're a public figure," she said. "Your records are your public records, but, at the same time, I can't say that I regret it because I got the best gift that life and God could give me, which are my children from that relationship."

José's attorney, Richard Poland, put on an aggressive defense attack, requesting a dismissal of the case on the grounds that his client had been denied his right to a speedy trial. In his defense arguments, Poland would take particular shots at Jenni, saying the allegations against José were filed for publicity purposes.

"It is the defense position that the entire case was brought to revive a rather mediocre singing career by the mother of one of the victims."

The tension in the court was made worse by the fact that José's family as well as Rivera's family were both present at the preliminary trial hearings. Angry stares and occasional words early in the proceedings led to a scuffle between the two families in the hallway outside the courtroom. The judge immediately ordered more security, insisted the families sit on opposite sides of the courtroom and that they leave the courtroom separately.

Once the trial began, tensions shot to an even higher level.

It was a grueling ordeal. At points in the trial, Jenni's daughter, Janney, and her sister, Rosie, were called to testify in graphic detail what José had done to them. "It was difficult for my girl, my daughter to be in front of a jury of 12 people and for her to have to say 'my father did this to me'," she told *Aquí y Ahora*. "And for my sister as well."

Emotions ran high during the trial and Jenni and her family members often had to be admonished by the judge for their outbursts. These outbursts from the family, as well as the rumors that José was allegedly targeted to be killed before the trial's conclusion, resulted in heightened security in the courtroom during the trial and sentencing phase.

"We were sometimes a problem," apologized Jenni in a story reported by the Associated Press. "Because, I guess, there was so much emotion involved."

On May 9, 2007, a jury convicted José of eight felony counts of lewd acts upon a child, oral copulation of a child, aggravated sexual assault, and continuous sexual assault. On June 21, 2007, Superior Court Judge Joan Comparet-Cassani sentenced José to 31 years to life in prison for his crimes.

In a conversation with Univision, Jenni recalled feeling a flood of emotions while sitting in the courtroom. "It's really hard to explain how I felt," she said. "Sadness, anger, pity. I was very moved when I saw him again after so many years. I couldn't even believe that this had happened."

After the conclusion of the sentencing hearing, Jenni was mentally exhausted and relieved that the decade-old ordeal was over.

"I'm glad it's over," she said in an Associated Press story.

Not long after her ex-husband was sentenced, Jenni took the stage at the Kodak Theater and celebrated the sentencing of her ex-husband with a packed house. "At one point, she brought out a bottle of cognac and drank a toast to her ex-husband who had just been put away," recalled Wald in a 2012 interview. "She took it for granted that everybody in the audience had been following the story and, in her mind, they were all going to celebrate his going to jail for life together."

The week after the trial ended, "Mi vida loca" was released. It was a breakthrough on a number of levels. Critics fell all over themselves praising the album for its toughness and street-level emotion. And indeed, "Mi vida loca" was very street, with Jenni's tales of real-world deceits and disappointments told in a style that was the musical equivalent of Latin women sitting around bitching about the wrongs in their lives.

"My life has been very crazy and difficult," Jenni said in a *Spanish Town* story alluding to the album. "I think I've lived happily. Difficult but happily."

Of major importance was that "Mi vida loca" became Jenni's first album to crack the mainstream *Billboard* Top 200 Album charts. Granted, it only topped out at number 113. But it was a sign that Jenni was beginning to enlarge her fan base beyond the niche

Latino market, and was poised to take on the rest of the world.

However, the good vibes of a career on the rise were once again interrupted by the antics of yet another ex-husband, Juan López. López was found guilty of drug trafficking and was sentenced to a long jail sentence. Still, Jenni was as good as her word, making regular visits to the jail with her children.

"I felt pride for being able to say that I did that for him," she told *Aquí y Ahora*.

Given the breakthrough nature of "Mi vida loca", it came as a surprise that Jenni would follow up that same year with two more albums, "La Diva en vivo" (The Diva Live) and "La Diva con banda sinaloense" (The Diva With Sinaloa Banda), which caused many to question the singer's judgment. "La Diva en vivo", her third live album in a year, was essentially dead on arrival at a time when most Spanish-language radio playlists were dominated by studio recordings. "La Diva con banda sinaloense" was a solid, if ultimately unspectacular collection, which found itself competing against Jenni's more established songs for radio time.

There were grumblings among some critics that Jenni was looking to flood the market and, by association, dilute the impact of "Mi vida loca" . Right or wrong, it seemed almost certain that Jenni had her mind on other things besides music.

As it turned out, she did.

CHAPTER ELEVEN

SEX WITH A PROPER STRANGER

Sometime during 2007, Jenni took a lover.

Who it was has never been revealed, although speculation is that the man was a musician in Jenni's touring band. What was known is that it was an affair, pure and simple, with not a whole lot of love involved.

"I wasn't in love," Jenni told Spanish-language journalist Cristina Saralegui of her affair. "But there was a lot of affection and I was trusting."

As these kinds of transitional relationships go, the affair between Jenni and her mystery lover lasted fifteen months before the couple split and went their separate ways. There was most certainly a measure of heartache and disappointment on Jenni's part . But in the wake of the breakup, everything seemed normal in Jenni's world.

All of that would change on October 17, 2008.

When Jenni received an early morning wakeup call from her record label's director of promotions, notifying her that a reported sex tape of her and a mystery man had been sent to an assortment of people in the music industry. Jenni was stunned and initially tried to play the call off as a joke. But she knew the reality of the reported sex tape. She had willingly made it with her then-boyfriend. When her manager, Gabriel Vázquez, called five minutes later, she confessed the truth to him.

"It wasn't just someone that you lie down with and film," she told Cristina. "It was a relationship that I maintained for a year and three months. I was in a relationship with him and I was trusting of him. He wanted that (the tape) and I gave it to him."

Jenni admitted to *Aquí y Ahora* that it was her nature to jump headlong into any relationship and that was what ultimately resulted in the sex tape being made. "It was his desire that he had (to make a sex tape) and I made it happen for him."

Jenni revealed only two copies of the tape existed. She had one and her lover had the other. Initially, she thought that perhaps her copy had been stolen during a break-in at her home some months earlier. However, a thorough search of her home produced her copy, which meant her mystery lover had to be the one who leaked the tape. Jenni called the mystery man and confronted him. He denied having done anything with his copy but Jenni wasn't buying it.

"I've lived with this shame and he needs to also," she told Cristina Saralegui. "The public needs to know who the despicable person who did this to me is."

Jenni wasted little time in getting the authorities in both the United States and Mexico involved (the tape was allegedly made in Mexico). Jenni's quick and decisive assault on the man who had betrayed her would go the legal route and that scared him to death. The mystery lover was now real concerned as illegally distributing the tape carried a possible sentence of 19 years in prison. As of December, Jenni seemed willing to sit back and let the legal system take its course.

Jenni admitted to *Aquí y Ahora* that she was extremely hurt and embarrassed by the situation. "I had to explain it to my children, to my siblings, parents, and friends. So yes, it hurt me very much."

A particular hurt was revisited when Jenni's former lover, somebody who she still had feelings for, reappeared on the scene and actually joined Jenni and her daughter when they were searching for the tape.

"We weren't together at the time but we were talking about things, sharing, and taking care of matters that we had to fix," she told Cristina. "I took him into my office, sat him down, and explained the whole thing to him. We were not lovers anymore but we were still in love.

"You can only imagine the pain."

The sex tape revelation would not be Jenni's only brush with infamy in 2008.

They loved Jenni in Raleigh, North Carolina. The Disco Rodeo nightclub was packed the night of June 21. It was hot, sweaty, packed to the rafters. It was a typical Jenni show. The beer was flowing freely. Jenni was in prime form, whipping the crowd into a frenzy. It was not a question of how out of control things would get. It was only a matter of when.

At 1:38 a.m., an overly intoxicated fan leaped onto the stage right in the middle of a song and was immediately set upon by security guards who began to roughly remove him. Jenni saw what was going on and stopped singing, and tried to get the guards to let the fan go. The highly intoxicated crowd, not understanding why Jenni had stopped singing, began booing Jenni. A barrage of beer bottles and other objects sailed at the stage.

Before Jenni could get out of the way, a beer bottle struck Jenni on the leg. An infuriated Jenni screamed out into the audience, demanding to know who threw the bottle. A man named Oscar Alexander Paz sheepishly yelled out that it was him. Jenni completely lost it. She demanded that the security guards grab Paz and bring him to the stage.

"He threw it at me," she told *Aquí y Ahora*. "I asked 'Who was it?' He said 'It was me.' So I told him to come up on the stage."

After verbally berating him, Jenni hit him square in the face with her diamond-encrusted microphone. Deep cuts appeared around his eyes and the blood began to flow. Jenni screamed defiance into the audience, as reported by *Qué Más*.

"I don't give a crap if you put this on YouTube! This is my stage and here I do whatever the hell I want!"

The dazed and bloodied Paz managed to stagger off the stage. He immediately called the local police to report that he had just been assaulted. Jenni had barely completed the concert and was walking backstage when she was approached by the local police, who promptly placed her in handcuffs and arrested her for assault. After spending several hours in the local jail, Jenni was released on $3,000 bail and ordered to appear in court on July 25. Jenni never made the court date but publicly apologized to the fan and made amends by inviting Paz out to Los Angeles for a concert as her guest.

Jenni sensed that her feisty, combative, tough-girl image was beginning to take on a life of its own and was quick to make an apology of sorts as reported by *People en Español.* "The only thing I can say is that I am not very happy about it. But I do take responsibility for what I've done."

Ever the businesswoman, Jenni found an opportunity to make public as well as financial gain out of the incident as she laughingly explained to *Aquí y Ahora.* "I put my jail mugshot on T-shirts and my children went to my concerts and sold them for $20 each."

CHAPTER TWELVE

ESSENTIALS AND NONESSENTIALS

Heading into 2008, Jenni was nothing if not prolific.

Whether it was her business side telling her to rush new albums out as a cash grab or a desire to just get in the studio and create, the new year kicked off with a daring move in which three albums on her father's Cintas Acuario label were released seemingly within moments of each other in January.

Jenni could have a good time in the studio. But she was also known as a performer who did not like to waste time. How quickly these three albums were recorded, and as more than one observer speculated, whether all three albums were recorded in one massive session, was not certain.

The result was a whole lot of nothing really spectacular, although nothing necessarily bad.

"Reyna, Reyna" (Queen, Queen), "No vuelvo ni de chiste" (There's No Way I'm Coming Back) and "Éxitos con banda mariachi norteño" (Banda Mariachi Norteño Hits) were all easily accessible, well done and, by degrees, ingratiating albums. Nothing anyone would be embarrassed to have in their CD collection but there was a definite sense of nonessential efforts designed to cash in hovering over the releases—which, given the flighty state of popular music, made perfect business sense.

What made news in this flood of music was the fourth album of 2008. "Jenni". It was an important step for Jenni in that, for the first time, she stepped forward as the producer, handling all the production behind the scenes and, in a very large sense, turning the knobs and giving the orders. The result was a good if ultimately not spectacular album.

However, Jenni was pragmatic and very businesslike in her reasoning for going behind the scenes for the first time. She envisioned a future where she might want to get out of the recording end of the business and wanted to position herself as a go-to producer for other artists. "Jenni" was a lot of things, but once the dust settled on how good an album it was, it was ultimately a calling card.

But like all of Jenni's previous Fonovisa releases, even the minor nature of "Jenni" proved a major hit. It would debut at number one on the top selling album lists in seven countries, including the U.S. Top Latin Albums list, making her the first Latin artist to have all of her major label releases debut at number one. The first single off the album, "Culpable o inocente," (Guilty or Innocent) would also do quite well.

Nobody was saying so publicly, but "Jenni" was most definitely a turning point for the singer. Yes, the album was most certainly catering to her loyal fan base but upon repeated listening, it becomes evident that Jenni was tinkering with a more polished, commercial pop sensibility and pointing toward a time when mainstream America would sit up and take notice.

Flushed with this success, Jenni took what she considered an important first step toward expanding her audience when she did a remix on the Britney Spears hit "Womanizer" for Mexican iTunes, which would premiere In November 2008. Once again, what many viewed as a trifle vanity project was actually a calculated move. Jenni most certainly saw the advantages of being tied to one of the most popular English-language pop singers in the world. It would get the word out to both fans and potential future collaborators that Jenni Rivera was around and, for the right situation, available.

Needless to say, Jenni was on the minds of the Latin music industry when it was awards season. Premio lo Nuestro voted the singer Top Female Artist of the Year . The *Billboard* Latin Music Awards awarded Jenni Regional Mexican Album of the Year' for the album "Mi vida loca" and Regional Mexican Airplay of the Year for the song "Mírame" (Look at Me) . Jenni received a Latin Grammy nomination for Best Ranchero Album for the album "La Diva en vivo" while Premios de la Radio once again honored Jenni as Best Solo Female of the Year.

To a very large degree, Jenni had come through scandal with her creativity intact.

CHAPTER THIRTEEN

BUSTED

In February 2007, Jenni finally achieved the American Dream. She bought her own home.

After a whirlwind seven-day escrow period, Jenni laid down $3.3 million for a massive home in Encino, California. Coming from humble beginnings, Jenni was amazed the first time she looked upon the 9,527-square-foot home, situated on four acres of land, and containing seven bedrooms and eleven bathrooms.

But before Jenni and her children moved in, Jenni took her family back to the old Long Beach neighborhood and stood in front of the garage . Jenni didn't want her children to forget where they had come from, and where they were now.

Jenni's popularity in Mexico had been part and parcel of her growing success, so she took every opportunity to travel to the country for the occasional concerts and promotional appearances. She made a trip to Mexico in May, 2009, to appear on a local television program. Jenni was in good spirits when she finally said goodbye to her friends and fans on May 23 to return to the Mexico City Airport and a return flight to

Los Angeles.

As reported by the *Latin American Herald Tribune*, Jenni was getting ready to board her flight when she declared to customs officials that she was taking $20,000 in cash back to the States. But when she opened her handbag, security officials discovered that there was $52,167 in her purse. She was immediately arrested on suspicion of attempting to smuggle the large amount of cash out of the country. Her bags were thoroughly searched and then Jenni was allowed to return to the U.S., pending further investigation into the matter by the Mexican government. Jenni would later acknowledge that the money in question had come from three shows she had done in Mexico City.

Ultimately Jenni was cleared of any wrongdoing. But the incident began to question Jenni's frequent trips across the border. One of the more outrageous speculations was that Jenni, either through threats or by her own volition, had entered into a pact with a drug cartel to regularly smuggle money into the U.S. for them.

Jenni would vehemently deny any and all accusations that she had illegal ties to criminals. Eventually the rumor and speculation died out. But Jenni was never far from the spotlight and controversy. In 2009, sadness would take its turn when her ex husband Juan came down with pneumonia while in prison and died in jail. Jenni was fighting back tears as she talked about the death of her second husband to *Aqui y Ahora*.

"I didn't know he was going to get sick in that prison," she said. "He died a prisoner, handcuffed to a hospital bed."

It would be a tough few days for Jenni, trying to comfort her two youngest children over the death of their father as well as dealing with her own emotions. That same week she was also contracted to do a concert in San Diego. Ever the trouper, Jenni, accompanied by her children and her father, put on a first-rate performance, highlighted by her son, Johnny, sitting in on the drums for several songs. But the death of her second husband weighed heavily on the singer and, at one point, she told the audience, "For me and my son, we're living through something very difficult."

Jenni would often comment on how she had a long memory when it came to somebody doing her dirty, and that memory was most certainly jogged in 2009, when while walking down a street in Mexico, she came face to face with the former lover who had released the infamous sex tape. Jenni saw red, ran up to the surprised man, and began beating him senseless. By the time the dust settled and cooler heads had pulled Jenni off him, the ex -lover was sporting a black eye and a bloody, broken lip.

By August, Jenni was involved in another round of drama when singer Graciela Beltrán accused Jenni's father of not paying her royalties on records released through his company. It was not long before Jenni had gotten drawn into the melee. Words were exchanged. Lawsuits were threatened. Eventually the feud between the two women died out. Publicly, Jenni held no grudges. It was just the latest round of drama in her life.

Jenni's children had grown into fairly well-adjusted kids despite the dysfunction and drama in their lives. Janney seemed poised to follow her mother into some aspect of the entertainment business. Jacqueline, who had recently made Jenni a grandmother with the birth of a daughter, Jaylah Hope, was studying nursing. Michael was in barber school. Jenicka was maintaining good grades in private school and Jennie's youngest, Johnny, would tell anyone who would listen that he was going to be the next Steven Spielberg.

Jenni had long been tempted to give acting a try and, in 2009, took a tentative step forward when she made her motion picture debut in "Addicted To Salsa," an English-language Robert Rodríguez film that told the story of a heroin-addicted salsa singer. Very little is actually known about the film except that it was released very briefly on television. Jenni is listed in the cast with no character name and she has chosen not to talk about the film.

Jenni was determined to stay active. She was insistent that she get some new music out to the fans and her label was more than willing to oblige. The first "Jenni: Super Deluxe" was a repackaging of the previous year's album that contained three new songs and a bonus DVD. One of the new tracks, the very tough and empowering "Ovarios" (Ovaries) broke out as an immediate single and was racing up the Top 40 within two weeks.

Her eleventh studio album, "La Gran Señora" (The Grand Dame), proved to be a step back of sorts. Rather than continue to play to her commercial banda musical strengths, Jenni saw fit to shift moods and go strictly mariachi and ranchera. As typified by the album's first single, "Ya lo sé" (I Already Know It), shifting to a more traditional side was a good idea, one that showed Jenni as not only a performer who was willing to slip and slide around the Mexican music template but also as somebody who could fly in the face of commercial expectations at the drop of a hat.

The singer related in an *El Paso Times* conversation that the genesis of "La gran señora" was her childhood, one preoccupied with the music of traditional Mexico and, in particular the mariachi and ranchera styles. "I hated getting up at five in the morning to set up our swap meet tables. But what I did love was playing that music."

Jenni spent quite a bit of time in preproduction in selecting just the right material. "I selected each title, considering not only how to sing it but also how to interpret it," she commented on her website, jenniriveramusic.com. "I recorded each song with passion and feeling."

It was that passion that was again on industry voters' minds when awards season came around. Despite her best efforts, Jenni was still frustrated by her attempts to break beyond Spanish-language music and into the mainstream English landscape. But Jenni took encouragement from the fact that the Latino wing of the industry had taken her to their hearts. *Billboard* proved extremely supportive, offering up nominations for Hot Latin Song Female for the song "Culpable o inocente", Hot Latin Song Female for the song "Inolvidable" (Unforgettable), Regional Mexican Airplay Song of the Year for the song "Culpable o inocente", Regional Airplay Song of the Year Female' for the song "Inolvidable", Top Latin Album of the

Year for "Jenni", Regional Mexican Album of the Year for "Jenni" and Tropical Song of the Year for the song "Cosas del amor" (Things of Love).

Her passion for playing live would continue through the year. Highlights included her two sold-out shows at the Nokia Amphitheater in Los Angeles and another sold-out performance in Acapulco at the Grand Forum Imperial.

In a *Billboard* feature, Jenni made no bones about her joy in performing. "When you get up on the stage and hear the applause, that's what makes you addicted to this (performing)."

CHAPTER FOURTEEN

REALITY IMPERFECT

Jenni had gotten used to the idea of being alone.

She could go out when and where she wanted. She did not have to let anyone know where she was going. It had been two years since there was a man in her life and that had ended in calamity. Perhaps more battle-scarred than anyone realized, Jenni had made it plain in several interviews that she would never marry again. But often in the same breath, she would hint that if the right person came along, she was more than willing to take another chance.

That chance presented itself during a series of concerts in Mazatlán. Sitting in the audience was Esteban Loaiza, a former Major League Baseball pitcher for several teams, including the Dodgers and the Yankees. At the time, he was playing in a Mexican league for a team based in Mazatlán and was the local celebrity.

During her performance, it was announced that Loaiza was in the audience. At the crowd's insistence, Loaiza stepped to the stage, said hello, and shook Jenni's hand. The crowd went wild, encouraging the pair to kiss.

"We did not kiss," Jenni recalled in a *Latina* interview. "We just said hi."

However there was a flicker of interest in Jenni's eyes, one that would intensify after the show when Jenni, who normally avoided after-show parties, agreed to make an appearance. Among the guests was Loaiza. The pair began to talk about their lives and their careers. Jenni was impressed that Loaiza was not overly impressed by celebrity and seemed a very down-to-earth person. Jenni would later explain to *Aquí y Ahora* that she was amazed he would take any interest in her at all.

"I'm very happy knowing that a gentleman took notice of this imperfect person," she said. "I have five children. I have a very difficult career, a public one. Lots of problems that have become scandals."

Jenni and Esteban kept in touch. They soon began dating and it was not long before Jenni was very much in love.

On the surface it seemed that Jenni had finally found Mr. Right. He was comfortable with Jenni constantly being in the spotlight and was great with her kids. And coming from a professional baseball background, Esteban was no stranger to unorthodox, unpredictable lifestyles.

Another record was on the horizon, and initially it looked like it would be another studio album. But both Jenni and Fonovisa looked back at the tapes of Jenni's 2009 Nokia Theater performances and agreed those shows had been truly magic nights. So it was decided that a projected May release should be another live album, "La Gran Señora en vivo" (The Grand Dame

Live). The album would not make the charts but it did prove a valuable memento of a time when Jenni, in a live setting, was at the height of her performing prowess.

Jenni did not let on that there was another bit of recording taking place that year. During her rare free moments, Jenni was sneaking off to the recording studio and recording a series of English-language pop songs. What kind of songs they were remained a mystery. But years later, in a *Los Angeles Times* interview, Gustavo López hinted at what might have been going on.

"It was always her dream to do an English album but she always thought that it would come in time," he said. "She always wanted to do an oldies album. She wanted to go back and do those songs and show people that she could do more than banda and mariachi music. She said that when the time came to do it, she would know it."

Jenni had become very media savvy during the course of her career. She knew the media sought her out because, quite simply, her name meant ratings and ratings meant money. That was why, when representatives of the fledgling cable television channel Mun2 approached her with the idea of creating a reality series a few years earlier, she considered it, but said no.

"I didn't want to bring it out at that time because I was single with five children and they were younger. I didn't like the idea of doing something that they would not agree with."

But when they approached her again in 2010, she had had a change of heart. *The Hollywood Reporter* initially reported the deal was for Jenni to star in a telenovela called *No Me Hallo* (Finding Myself). Jenni was not ready to invest the kind of time required and deal with the logistics that appearing the show would require. Besides, she had another idea.

Jenni Rivera Presents Chiquis a Raq C would focus on Jenni's daughter, Janney, and her friend, Racquel Córdova, as they went about their day-to-day business lives, talked about boys, and watched as Janney handles the various professional and domestic duties as Jenni's manager. Jenni would act as executive producer and make sporadic appearances, both informally and in a concert setting.

"This show is very real," Jenni told *Latina*. "And that's what's going to make it very interesting. This is the first show produced by Latin people for Latin people."

Throughout much of the summer, cameras were Jenni's constant companion as she monitored the day-to-day progress of the show. Mun2 had been so taken with the concept that they ordered twelve episodes. It was a nonstop odyssey in which cameras were always in their lives, recording the important and minor moments in the lives of the two women as centered around the personal and professional life of Jenni.

Initially it was only going to be Jenni as producer with her daughter and friend as the program's focus. But as Flavio Morales recalled in *The Hollywood Reporter*, "One day Jenni got the bug."

"One day she gave Janney the day off (from filming) and did the 5:30 wakeup call with the trainer, making the breakfast and getting the kids off to school and so on. She realized what we all knew. That she was a natural. Her ability to come up with really quick sound bites was very real."

It was a crazy time for Jenni and her family. With cameras on them from the moment they got up until the moment they went to bed, every moment was subject to the camera's eye. There was little that was off limits. Happily Jenni and her family adjusted quickly and became comfortable with the intrusion. Over the course of twelve episodes, they had become reality show pros.

Jenni had taken a very big risk by putting her children on television and in the public eye. Her kids had already experienced the downside of celebrity with their mother's very public personal drama and scandal. Putting them squarely in the spotlight could have done a lot of damage. Fortunately, Jenni's children never felt this was something their mother was making them do and considered their day-to-day interactions with the ever-present camera a big adventure. There were moments when Jenni, who was also juggling a recording and touring career, would have relished a day off. But the excitement and enthusiasm kept her going.

Jenni Rivera Presents Chiquis And Raq C made its television debut on July 3 and was an instant critical and ratings success. Mun2 was definitely interested in more. And Jenni definitely had another idea.

I Love Jenni seemed a natural jumping-off point from *Jenni Rivera Presents Chiquis And Raq C.* Whereas the first show focused primarily on her daughter and friend with Jenni making only occasional appearances, *I Love Jenni* would focus on the entire family as they went through the personal and professional moments that surrounded a family whose matriarch happened to be a big star. Jenni initially called the concept of *I Love Jenni* as a kind of homage to the classic *I Love Lucy* television series, with an emphasis on the crazy side of life. But Jenni predicted in a *Latina* conversation that the Mexican audience would get much more out of it.

"I want to be able to tell the truth about who Jenni is as a human being, a mother, a wife, as a friend, and as an artist," she said. "I'm going to take it as my opportunity to tell the truth."

By the time her first show premiered in July, Jenni and her family were already hard at work on the first season of *I Love Jenni* . Similar to the previous show, Jenni and her family continued to have cameras on them all the time. Discussions serious and humorous, situations dramatic and comedic, real emotions on display—it was all recorded for posterity through the camera's eye. Jenni admitted Esteban had not bargained for being part of a television show and was a bit uncomfortable at first but he adjusted very quickly and really seemed to be enjoying himself.

Adding even more to her already full plate, Jenni continued to tour sporadically through the months of June, July, and August, wowing audiences in Hollywood in the States and playing to sold-out crowds in Guadalajara, Monterrey, Acapulco, and Puebla in Mexico.

Midway through the year, Jenni was approached with the opportunity to once again stretch her acting muscles in a low-budget, very Latin-flavored drama called *Filly Brown* . The role of an incarcerated mother of an aspiring rap singer was small, only four scenes, and the filmmakers were almost certain Jenni would not want to do it. However Jenni saw strength in the role. It also did not hurt that the film would also be starring Edward James Olmos and Lou Diamond Phillips. Of course there was also the opportunity to spread her growing brand into the acting arena. Jenni agreed to do the film, which was set to begin shooting in January 2011.

Meanwhile the romance between Esteban and Jenni had blossomed. The couple would occasionally talk about marriage but nothing definite was decided—until the day Esteban, in a truly romantic gesture, gathered Jenni and all her children together, proposed, and gave her a ring. Jenni said yes. The only problem was coming up with a date to tie the knot. Finally, in August, the couple agreed to a September 8 ceremony, which would take place at The Hummingbird Nest Ranch in Simi Valley, California.

The famed designer Eduardo Lucero designed a beautiful gown for Jenni as well as the clothes for the bridesmaids and Esteban. More than eight hundred guests attended the wedding and watched as Esteban and Jenni danced their first dance as a married couple to the song "El amor" (The Love) sung by famed Latino singer Tito "El Bambino".

Things ran relatively smoothly that day. The only difficulty was that a woman and her daughter had somehow managed to get through security and the woman, at one point, was becoming a nuisance when she was begging Janney to let her daughter sing for her mother on her special day. But since Jenni noticed her son, Michael, and the daughter seemed to be getting along, she chose not to make a scene.

"I was really a Queen for a day," she reported to *Latina*. "I was happy as a single woman and I'm happy as a married woman."

Speculation would immediately run wild that Jenni would celebrate this new man in her life by having a sixth child. Jenni was quick to laughingly dismiss the rumor when she told *Latina*, "I am not pregnant and I don't plan on getting pregnant ever again."

Jenni's happiness would extend to the awards season as the Latin music industry once again chose to honor her creative achievements. *Billboard* honored Jenni for the third year in a row for Best Female Regional Mexican Artist of the Year . She was a Premios lo Nuestro winner for Best Female Artist of the Year and was nominated for Best Regional Mexican Artist . Finally Jenni was a multiple nominee for Mariachi Song of the Year, Solo Woman of the Year and Personality of yhe Year by Premios de la Radio.

By year's end she would also find time for a rare collaboration. Long an admirer of superstar Ricky Martin, she was happily surprised when Martin rang her up for some help. The singer was toying with the idea of including the song "Lo mejor de mi vida eres tú" (The Best Thing in My Life is You) and was looking for a banda vibe for the tune which would appear on his album "Musica+Alma+Sexo." Needless to say, the pair made beautiful music together and it whet Jenni's appetite to work with other artists more often.

A month after her wedding, Jenni and Esteban brought her family together for dinner. Everything was pleasant and cordial. However, Jenni kept noticing Michael kept getting cell phone calls during dinner. She also noticed he had a worried expression on his face.

"I asked my son, 'What do you have going on? What's happening?'" she recalled to *Aquí y Ahora*.

Michael was being evasive and nervous, refusing to give her a straight answer. Jenni let it drop until later that night, when Michael dropped by the house unexpectedly.

"He told me that the phone calls were from the mother of a young woman who was very upset and that the lady wanted to speak to me."

CHAPTER FIFTEEN

HERE COMES TROUBLE

Jenni refused to talk to the woman. But she did find out what was going on.

Shortly after the mother and daughter crashed her wedding, Michael and the young girl began dating. Eventually they began having sex. Michael was nineteen at the time. The girl was sixteen.

In the ensuing weeks, Jenni would hear through her people that the mother wanted some kind of compensation from Jenni, inferring that the whole situation could go away if Jenni paid the woman money. Jenni refused.

Midway through December, five police cars and nearly a dozen police officers and detectives pulled up in front of Jenni's house, put Michael in handcuffs, and took him to jail on the charge of having sex with a minor. Jenni was upset at witnessing the scene. Once she stopped being upset, she was amazed at the very real show of force she witnessed.

"To arrest someone who had sex with someone, with their consent, who is a minor?" she told *Aquí y Ahora*. "He wasn't a rapist. He wasn't a serial killer.

He wasn't someone with a criminal record."

Michael was taken to the Robert Presley Correctional Center in Riverside County, California. He was arraigned on charges of sexual misconduct with a minor and released on $50,000 bail, pending trial. Never one to shy away from scandal, Jenni called a press conference to talk about her son's arrest and the charges against him.

Jenni took the brave step of acknowledging to the assembled press that, according to the law, nobody under the age of eighteen can give consent to have sexual relations. She further said, "So if something had happened, my son knew that the girl was a minor, then I am in complete agreement that he needs to pay for the crime." She further defended her parenting skills by indicating she was not the kind of mom who lets her kids do whatever they want.

Jenni continued her march toward the start of filming on *Filly Brown* . She knew that despite the acting and theatrics of her live performances, acting in movies was a whole different game. And so she spent a month learning how to act for the camera. By the end of the year, her directors and co-stars felt confident the novice actress was ready for her close-up.

Jenni made it through the end of 2010 relatively unscathed by all the scandal and drama. But shortly after the first of the year, Jenni came down with a kidney ailment. And just like everything else surrounding the singer's life, we knew because she Tweeted the prognosis, as only Jenni could, from her hospital bed.

"I can't stand up! My kidneys are fucked! It's awful to be so messed up. I have a 103-degree fever. I feel horrible. But I have to feel better by tomorrow. I will be meeting with Lou Diamond Phillips and Edward James Olmos. We start filming January 10."

Jenni recovered in time to shoot her scenes for *Filly Brown* and, according to a *Los Angeles Times* article, she was too good to be true as an actress and a human being. After discovering the set still photographer was having financial difficulties, Jenni went to the filmmakers and insisted her fee for the film go to him. When a crew member happened to mention that a family member was a Jenni fan, the singer returned to the set the next day with a signed photo and a CD for that person. As an actress, Jenni was reportedly instinctive in assessing her character, played well with the emotions of an incarcerated mother attempting to reach out to her daughter, and, according to her directors and co-stars, showed exceptional acting ability for somebody with so little experience.

"I had to dig deep for that one," Jenni would tell a packed press conference in November. "I think you'll be pleasantly surprised. If I can make Edward James Olmos cry, to me that means it was a success."

March saw Jenni and her family going full bore in the filming of *I Love Jenni*. It was at that point, mere months into her marriage, that the first rumors of Esteban's infidelity began to appear in *Qué Más* and other outlets. It was but a minor irritant to Jenni, who felt she knew her husband well enough to not believe the reports.

March would also bring a conclusion to the heart-wrenching ordeal of her son Michael's sex charges . After the trial, in which Michael pleaded guilty to the charge of having sex with a minor, Jenni's son was found guilty of that charge but two additional charges of sexual abuse with a minor were dropped. Michael was fined $600 and ordered to wear an electronic monitoring device for ninety days. He did not have to register as a sex offender.

On the way out of the courtroom, a relieved Jenni told the assembled press, "I'm happy, happy. I'm thanking justice. My son should have done better but what happens, happens."

CHAPTER SIXTEEN

KNOCK DOWN, DRAG OUT

Fortunately, there was a lot of good on the horizon to counteract the bad.

In the midst of her son's trial, *I Love Jenni* premiered on March 6, 2011. Like the previous show, *I Love Jenni* immediately captured the fascination of the Mexican audience. The ratings, by Mun2 standards, were very good. Jenni and her family were alternately funny and serious but, most importantly, real. Shows like *I Love Jenni* rise or fall based on their relatability, and people were definitely relating.

The nature of the show allowed Jenni to be her outspoken, boisterous self. It was a shock to many, especially in the episode where Jenni sent one of her daughters off for the day by saying, "Have a good day and don't get pregnant."

But as she said in a *New York Times* article, people getting upset about what she said did not bother her. "It doesn't bother me at all that some people think that I am too outspoken. Actually, if they're thinking about me, it bothers them. But they'll get over it."

Barely a handful of episodes into the first season and the Mun2 people were already making plans for a second.

However, while her television career was taking off, Jenni was not about to forget that she was a singer first and was soon making preparations to go back into the studio. Not surprisingly, she had her eye on both art and commerce.

"Joyas Prestadas" would be an all-covers album, paying homage to the great singers and songs that captivated her as a teenager. The songs would be primarily ballads, big and bold with thick, lush, dramatic production. Early on, Jenni decided to record two different versions of the album: one in traditional banda style and the other in a much more American/pop style. She reasoned that she would continue to cater to the traditional Mexican audience that had brought her so far, and at the same time, take that first deliberate—and yes, calculated—step toward cracking the U.S. market.

Throughout the year, Jenni would make a point of doing occasional shows on both sides of the border. Jenni's performances continued to be loud, wild, beer-fueled events. That, as she found out during a show in Puerto Vallarta, could easily get ugly.

Right in the middle of a song, a beer can thrown by a young woman suddenly sailed out of the crowd and struck Jenni. The singer went ballistic. Jenni screamed at the security people to wade into the audience and drag the young woman on stage. Jenni got in the woman's face.

"Throw at me, here, where I am," she screamed. "Throw it at me. Who do you think has the bigger balls, you or me?"

With that Jenni opened the beer can, poured the beer on the woman's head and, for good measure, yanked the young woman's hair several times before security took her offstage.

There was a bit of an uproar in the media, cries of alleged thug-like behavior on the part of the singer. Then it was over.

Until a few days later, when another concert in Guanajuato got out of hand. It seems word of the previous beer-throwing incident had gotten around and a segment of Jenni's fans began to think of it as a regular part of the show. Consequently, midway through this latest concert, another beer can came flying out of the audience, striking a member of Jenni's band. Jenni's brother, Juan, happened to be with her on this leg of the tour and he took it upon himself to defend his sister's honor. Security found the culprit and dragged him up on stage, where he was attacked by Juan, who punched him in the head several times, knocking him out. Juan and the security team then dragged the unconscious man off the stage.

Juan would later hold a press conference during which he apologized for his actions. But these beatings and fan assaults at Jenni's concerts were now prompting a groundswell of negative press. Jenni would occasionally address her actions. She would often say that what happened was a self-defense mechanism that kicked in whenever she felt she was being approached in a negative manner. But ultimately her response was as simple as, "I am the same as the public," she told The Associated Press. "I am the same as my fans."

But in a more reflective mood when interviewed by ABC/Univision, the singer conceded she did "have some work to do when it came to turning the other cheek."

However much publicized dust-ups with fans did not stop Jenni from being a top live attraction. She proved her drawing power in September when she became the first regional Mexican female singer to sell out the Staples Center in Los Angeles

Jenni was very much in the moment during the Staples Center concert. It was both a homecoming and a sign that Jenni had truly arrived at the pinnacle of stardom in the Latin American music scene. It showed in a concert that was fiery in its presentation and theatrical in its execution. The set list was all over the place; hardcore *norteños* and her *narcocorrido*-laced hits ran smoothly into songs set distinctively in the ranchero/mariachi/banda world. But what brought particular joy to the evening was that the audience was her people. The women were dressed in their party finery, yelling out encouragement and dancing in the aisles. The men in attendance were most certainly nodding and smiling, a sign that the male-dominated scene officially had a *comadre*. It was a night for the star and the real people to rejoice.

It would be a busy summer for Jenni on the business front. The early success of her reality programming resulted in Mun2 stepping up to the plate and signing Jenni to a long-term and very lucrative production deal. And there was satisfaction on all sides when Jenni and Fonovisa renewed their contract.

The much-anticipated "Joyas Prestadas" was released in November in both banda and pop formats.

The consensus was that Jenni was essentially critic proof at this point and that her fans would flock to any new Jenni music. And so while critics were generally positive in their reviews, the album was considered a trifle, a well-done, well-intentioned vanity project which, given her status as a star, she was definitely entitled to. Keen-eyed observers noted the pop elements and were quick to point to "Joyas Prestadas" as the first tentative step toward mainstream acceptance.

The week of the release, Jenni's rise to the level of superstardom was validated when, at a packed press conference at Universal City Walk at Universal City, California, she donated the multi-colored dress she wore on stage to the collection of memorabilia housed in the famed Hard Rock Café - the first time a Mexican female singer was honored with her donation to the collection.

Awards season once again saw Jenni in the spotlight. She was a multi-category nominee in the *Billboard* Latin Grammy balloting for Top Latin Album Female Artist of the Year, Regional Mexican Album of the Year for "La Gran Senora" and Regional Mexican Album Solo Artist of the Year.

Jenni ended the year in a comfort zone. She was a monster musical success, adored by her husband and her children. She had survived the controversies and scandal with her head held high. Jenni pretty much had it all.

But she knew there was still so much to do.

CHAPTER SEVENTEEN

WALKING THE WALK

Jenni's songs had always espoused equal rights, positive social images for women and children, and a very hard line against domestic violence and sexual abuse. But unlike many celebrities who "talked the talk" when a camera was on them but ultimately would not "walk the walk," Jenni's political and social stances went beyond the music into active participation in the real world.

After having experienced firsthand the horrors of spousal abuse and bearing witness to the sexual abuse of her daughter and sister, Jenni was quick to take up the cause, starting her own activist group, The Jenni Rivera Love Foundation, that put her willingly in the forefront of championing the rights of single mothers, young mothers, and those who have experienced sexual abuse and spousal violence.

Women's equality would always be at the forefront of Jenni's social agenda and she would take every opportunity and media outlet to get her point across, including radio. Beginning in 2010, Jenni began to host a four-hour weekly Spanish-language call-in radio show called "Contacto Directo con Jenni Rivera" in which Jenni preached the gospel of female empowerment and equality to Latinas.

Jenni's work gained national attention. On August 6, 2010, Jenni was named Los Angeles spokeswoman for the National Coalition Against Battered Women and Domestic Violence. A press release announcing the appointment said, "In her life, Jenni has fought for women's rights, for protection of children subject to abuse and had dedicated herself to the empowerment and protection of battered women everywhere." To honor her good works, the Los Angeles City Council passed a resolution marking the day of the appointment Jenni Rivera Day.

That same year, Jenni turned her activism in the direction of the wave of anti-immigration legislation that was sweeping the land. She took particular aim at a Senate bill making its way through the Arizona legislature, SB1070. Arizona had long been a hotbed of support for Jenni throughout her career and, in the spirit of payback, she ventured out in 110-degree temperature to march with the people during an anti-SB1070 rally. Jenni's star power was an immediate attraction for reporters covering the event. And, with the sweat dripping down her forehead, she was more than willing to make her opinion known.

"SB1070 is an injustice," she yelled out amid the sounds of protest. "It's discrimination! It doesn't respect humanity and it's racist."

Jenni marched five miles before succumbing to the heat and exhaustion. She spent some hours in a nearby hospital but emerged with her fighting spirit intact.

In October, 2011, Jenni turned her attention to the plight of lesbian, gay, bisexual, and transgendered youth. To reinforce her anti-bullying stance, she participated in a GLAAD (Gay & Lesbian Alliance Against Defamation) event and wore purple clothing, the rally color for gay rights, during Spirit Day, a day set aside for espousing gay rights. On the occasion of her appearance at the October 21, 2011, *Billboard* Latin Grammys, she was resplendent in a purple gown that signified her support of the cause to honor those LGBT people who had lost their lives to suicide because of bullying and other forms of harassment.

Jenni's causes were not only national in scope. When Jenni heard about the Long Beach-based nonprofit organization California Families in Focus, an organization dedicated to helping families escape the horrors of physical and mental abuse, she stepped right in to help. On one occasion she sent over a van full of toys for the children in need. On another, a van appeared full of pajamas and slippers for the women being helped by the program.

"When you are commended for giving back, it feels great," she commented to *the Long Beach Press Telegram* about her contributions to those in need. "When you are able to come out of poverty and difficulty and help other people, it is very satisfying."

Then there were those non-publicized human moments when Jenni showed she knew the real meaning of charity. There were the anonymous cash donations to pay for funerals and to help out a stranger who was ill. Jenni would often be approached by fans who would marvel at the very high-end earrings and bracelets she was wearing. Inevitably they would tell

Jenni that one of her earrings would probably pay their rent. Without hesitation she would take off an earring and give it to the person. The same with the bracelets. Jenni's generosity was playing havoc with her expensive tastes and she eventually took to wearing fake jewelry because all the real stuff had been given away to those in need.

Jenni lived in the fantasy world of entertainment. But her actions showed that she was very much a person of the streets—and of the people.

CHAPTER EIGHTEEN

ON THE VERGE

Entering 2012, Jenni had a love affair with television. It was enlarging her brand and slowly but surely inching the door open for wider mass acceptance. So when television continued to call, Jenni was quick to say yes.

A Mexican version of the mainstream U.S. talent show *The Voice* had begun production the previous year and had been an instant success. Going into 2012, the producers were looking for a bit more sizzle to liven up the show and increase viewership. The first person they thought of was Jenni. Jenni agreed to become a guest judge and mentor for the contestants on the show on a semi-regular basis. An occasional quick hop to Mexico to film her segments would fit in with her already busy schedule. This was a particular treat for Jenni because it allowed her to work alongside such respected Latin performers as Beto Cuevas, Paulina Rubio, and Miguel Bose.

The producers of *I Love Jenni* were always on the hunt for ways to incorporate Jenni into their primetime lineup. Jenni came up with an idea for a six-episode miniseries entitled *Chiquis In Control* that would focus on her daughter Janney as she lived her own life in New York while attempting to start a beauty salon. Jenni would end up appearing in five of the six episodes.

And when Jenni's second daughter, Jacqui, announced she was engaged to be married, Jenni took it upon herself to give her daughter the ultimate wedding present: *Jenni Rivera Presents: The Wedding Of My Daughter*, a one-hour special that would air in November and follow her daughter's odyssey to the wedding chapel.

Jenni had also recently taken the important step of signing with CAA, a major Hollywood talent agency, with an eye toward creating her own U.S. television show.

"The talk of her getting her own television show was a good idea," agreed author Elijah Wald. "I think the television show would have broken her through. As a character, Jenni could have broken through like crazy. I didn't see anybody out there who had the potential that Jenni had in that way."

Looking ahead to 2013, Jenni had already laid the groundwork for a number of business ventures that included a line of denim jeans, curling irons, and plans to open a series of boutique stores.

But at the end of the day, it was the music that got her there and she was reportedly taking steps to kick open the door with her next album, an all-out assault on the U.S. market with an all-English-language and very pop-oriented album. A lot of people in the music industry thought such a move was a slam dunk. In hindsight, Wald did not think that was going to work.

"I think she was going to do power ballads," he speculated on the proposed Americanized album. "When I interviewed Jenni, she said that there were thousands of women who sang like Celine Dion and so she decided to go the tough girl way. But once you try to crack the Anglo market, there are thousands of women who sing like Celine Dion and most of them are not heavy-set women in their forties. I don't think it would have been a stupid decision to do the album and I'm sure that a lot of people who were Jenni fans would have bought it."

Despite the fact that Jenni was full bore into her career in 2012, reality of a personal nature was never far behind. And so the entire population of Mexico was shocked to discover while watching an early-in-the-year episode of *I Love Jenni* when the singer disclosed that a lump had been discovered in her breast. Shock would turn to relief when the singer explained to her audience that the tumor was found to be non-cancerous and that she was monitoring the situation with regular examinations.

Jenni chronicled the ordeal as only Jenni could with equal parts candor and humor in a conversation with radio host Carson Daly. "Well, my boobs are fine now. It's one of those things that a lot of females go through. I went to get a mammogram and that's what they found. I had to go back to the hospital every six months. I went to the hospital and got it removed. It was one of the hardest times of my life."

What few realized at the time was the immense impact middle-aged Jenni was having on Mexican pop culture. Record labels now more than ever were seeking out what they hoped would be the next Jenni

Rivera. But it would be their idealized version of what Mexican pop singers should be, which was skinny women and dashing male Latin lover types. But Wald is convinced Jenni had something that any potential heirs to the throne would have to work very hard to duplicate.

"She never ran away from the tabloid stuff and the sensationalism. Her fans supported her no matter what. As far as she was concerned, the rest of the world could go to hell."

By the time the summer of 2012 came to a close, the consensus among observers was that Jenni's conquest of America was imminent.

As she said in the CNN Marquee Blog, she was thrilled with the success. "I'm very happy by the success that I've had. I worked so hard at it. It's not that I feel that I deserve it. You kind of work hard and you have expectations. So I'm living my expectations right now. It's great. It's beautiful."

CHAPTER NINETEEN

THE COMING STORM

Esteban Loaiza was light years away from what Jenni's first two husbands had been.

He was worldly, had been gainfully employed, and seemed content to stay in the background, only seeming to appear at some kind of event for Jenni. In fact, if it was not for his appearances on *I Love Jenni*, many would have thought Esteban was a figment of Jenni's imagination. The reality was that he was nurturing, good with the kids, and a constant source of love and support. On several occasions she would refer to Esteban as her Prince Charming.

On October 1, 2012, Jenni filed for divorce from Esteban Loaiza.

The cold, hard legalese of the divorce papers filed by Jenni had all been heard before. The court documents cited "irreconcilable differences" as the reason for ending the marriage. There was a pre-nuptial agreement in place. Jenni's publicist issued a statement that said "private circumstances occurred during the lapse of the two-year marriage."

To Jenni's legions of fans, the announcement was

both sad and perplexing. With no concrete reasons for the divorce forthcoming, it left the door open for the tabloid press to speculate on the causes of the divorce. Almost since they got together, there had been rumors that Esteban was being unfaithful and many immediately jumped to that conclusion as the reason for the divorce. Further down the gossip trail, it had been whispered that Esteban was gay. There were also reports that Esteban had been stealing money from Jenni.

Jenni had no problem setting the record straight in a candid conversation with *El Gordo y La Flaca*. She blasted the media for their rumor mongering and was quick to set the record straight that the cause of the divorce was not Esteban's alleged infidelities. She also made it very plain that, like all married couples, Esteban and she would often have discussions that would occasionally turn loud, but there was never any mistreatment, abuse, or physical violence. But while she refused to open up about the specific cause, she did lay down a timeline about what led to it.

Jenni had a sense in early September that something was not quite right. She confided those concerns to her sister Rosie. Jenni did not know exactly why she had those concerns but she was certain it was not her imagination and she set about investigating certain aspects of her business and professional world.

"Three weeks ago (early September), I noticed that things were not as they seemed," she told *El Gordo y La Flaca*. "On September 21, I noticed a couple of things and decided to investigate. On September 21, I asked him (Esteban) to leave my house."

The showdown between Esteban and Jenni was calm. There was no screaming. They simply spoke. Esteban was extremely apologetic. He was hoping that clearing the air surrounding his wrong doings would end in a reconciliation.

Jenni was in the midst of a tour at the time, but when the tour ended she immediately consulted her lawyers and filed for divorce. "I never should have married him," she raged during the *El Gordo y La Flaca* interview. "I suffered a lot and now I see it was a mistake. The things that happened were terrible, bad enough that I finally stood up and said, 'no more. I won't take this anymore."

But even as the divorce decree was filed and the media headlines blared, Jenni would remain surprisingly loyal to the man who had wronged her. "He's good and he's fair and it's not good for my honor if he looks bad," she explained in the *El Gordo y La Flaca* interview. "He said he should not have done those things and was insistent that we reconcile. I told him no way and that the divorce would be finalized in six months."

Although Jenni's comments seemed to indicate Esteban may well have been stealing money, nothing really specific was being said. And with Esteban unwilling to talk about it, the media continued its feeding frenzy, and came up with a story that was truly vicious.

According to tabloid reports, Jenni filed for divorce when she reportedly found out that her daughter Janney had been having an affair with Esteban. The reaction from Janney was immediate. On

October 25, Jenni's daughter took to Twitter to vehemently deny the rumor.

"Don't believe everything you read. I would never do that. It's a horrible accusation."

Jenni was cautious in defending her daughter. She was approached by media outlets for comment and refused. But she allegedly never came out and said she did not believe her daughter would do such a thing. Which is not to say she believed the rumors.

In his own quiet way, Esteban would fight back against the divorce and the outrageous speculation and rumors. He refused to sign and return the divorce papers filed by Jenni, which legally put him in jeopardy of forfeiting any rights to compensation from the divorce settlement. In a conversation with *El Gordo y La Flaca* he said, "Right now, I feel so down with everything that is happening right now. But I just have to move forward. A lot of things are being said that just aren't true."

In typical Jenni fashion, the singer chose to face the divorce issue head on and went public with an official statement on the matter that she hoped would end the three-ring circus of tabloid media attention. "Friends. I don't want to make a spectacle out of this. This divorce is just like any other divorce. I promise that I will continue being a strong mother, one that works hard and always defends her children. To me this is not a failure rather than another chapter in my life."

The timing of the divorce and subsequent accusation had come when the relationship between mother and daughter was already a bit strained. No reason was given for it being that way and many dismissed it as the age-old battle over parental control and a child seeking independence. Whatever the reason, Jenni and Janney were not speaking as often as they used to. And the fates were conspiring to complicate that relationship even further.

In early November, Jenni was on her way to a recording session for her radio show when she encountered Janney's boyfriend, Ángel del Villar, owner of Del Records, in the studio parking lot. An argument ensued and words were exchanged that Jenni interpreted as an insult. When Jenni got emotional, she usually let those emotions out on Twitter. This incident would prove no exception.

"What kind of man are you?," she Tweeted to Villar and to her daughter. "What makes you think it's okay to scream nasty things like that to a woman that's only shown you respect? You're a coward for having your bodyguards with you." And to her daughter she followed with, "Congrats to your boyfriend. Good job."

Janney's response was quick and equally angry. "You haven't given me the day or day. So how would you know if he were even still my boyfriend? And that's besides the point. We still have bigger and more important issues to resolve. I'm not defending him. That shouldn't have been said or done. But like I said, you should take the time to hear me out. After all I deserve it. I love you.

"Mom, you know how to get a hold of me."

CHAPTER TWENTY

BREAK ON THROUGH

Jenni's world was about to change.

On the surface it just seemed like Jenni's typical itinerary. A trip to Mexico for a series of concerts and to tape episodes of *The Voice: Mexico* . But in the days leading up to her departure, Jenni was suddenly the hot topic in Hollywood and, according to reports, was moments away from breaking through to U.S. stardom.

First came the announcement that the long-anticipated English-language album would be released sometime in 2013. Particulars were not available but it was noted that over the course of two relatively low-profile sessions in 2004 and 2010, there was already quite a bit of English-language material in the can. No matter the material's history, observers of the pop music and Latin music scenes made note of the importance of the release and, along with Jenni's fans, were anxiously waiting.

This would truly be a test of Jenni's popularity and the possibilities of staking a claim in the English-language world. Would the hardcore fans who had supported her all these years take offense at her sudden flight to mainstream American acceptance? Would the English-speaking world even know who she was, let alone be interested in her music? These were questions that would shortly have answers.

It had also been announced that the movie *Filly Brown*, after a good reception at the annual Sundance Film Festival, would hit theaters in April 2013 and, in particular, Jenni's performance was already being touted as a possible Best Actress contender for the Oscars.

Jenni's popularity on Mexican television also saw an interesting offer coming through to appear in a new Mexican telenovela entitled *Porque El Amor Manda*, based on a Colombian soap opera called *El Secretario*. Jenni readily accepted the role of a feisty, brave, tough woman whose character would appear periodically in selected episodes. The show's producer, Juan Osorio, as reported in lamajor.com, was so thrilled to have Jenni on the show in any capacity that he agreed to work around her schedule and her already contracted concert appearances and said she would be allowed to sing the show's theme song. Jenni was scheduled to begin filming in July 2013.

Jenni's notoriety from her Mun2 reality shows was also beginning to seep across the border. In a conversation with radio personality Carson Daly, she revealed, "They're kind of looking to throw me on *Celebrity Apprentice*. I'm more of a businesswoman than an artist so I would like to do it. And then they're also considering me for *Dancing with the Stars*. But we'll see."

Throughout September and October, Jenni's U.S. team was actively shopping a proposed television show to the major networks. To be sure, there was some reluctance and skepticism about a show starring a Mexican-American woman who nobody really knew about. But with the previous sitcom success of comic George López as an example, executives were at least listening.

By December, at least one network took the bait . It was announced that ABC television network had commissioned a television pilot for a possible TV sitcom entitled *Jenni* . Jenni and her manager Peter Saldago would serve as the show's producers and the show would be put together by executive producer Robert L. Boyette, who had been responsible for such classic television series as *Family Matters*, *Full House* and *Step by Step.* The show's premise would be largely autobiographical, starring Jenni as a strong-willed, middle-class, single Latina struggling to raise her family the right way while dealing with the rigors of running a family business and always-challenging relatives.

In her final press conference, Jenni laid out some of the particulars of what the show would be about. "Jenni is a single mother of three boys and a girl who split from her husband because he was an alcoholic. Jenni's father passes away and leaves her the family business, a cantina. I will sing at the cantina from time to time."

Jenni acknowledged to Carson Daly that she felt it was important that her reality television work and her upcoming ABC pilot had and would go beyond pure entertainment and that they would be getting an important message out to the Latino audience.

"I've always been very transparent with my fans

and this is obviously something they need to know how to handle in case they go through it," she explained. "So many people go through it and I believe that God gave me the opportunity to go through it, not because I'm a bad person. It's just that he needed an example for my people."

Wald held out high hopes for Jenni's budding television and movie career. But he also felt she was maturing as a concert performer despite what many would consider her advanced age of forty-three. "The last time I saw her at a club show, I felt that this was the ideal way for her to go because the kind of performance she was doing well into her sixties."

With all the new opportunities heading her way, Jenni could be forgiven for being a bit self-centered and ego-driven in the days leading up to her trip to Mexico. She Tweeted as much a few days before boarding the plane to Monterrey.

"I'm going to give them hell while I'm breathing."

CHAPTER TWENTY-ONE

TIMELINE TO TRAGEDY

At the moment the Mexican airport tower lost contact with the plane carrying Jenni and her entourage, it was reportedly flying over Sierra de Galeana, a wooded, somewhat mountainous area, approximately seventy-five miles south of Monterrey, Mexico.

In piecing together the timeline of what happened next, only one thing was certain. At the moment the tower lost contact with the plane carrying Jenni and her entourage, the plane was already in a vertical nosedive from a height of twenty thousand feet, traveling in excess of six hundred miles per hour.

"The plane practically nosedived," Secretary of Communication and Transportation Gerardo Ruiz Esparza told worldwide media in the hours following the crash. "It must have been terrible."

According to investigators, the plane hit the ground approximately 1.2 miles from the point where it began falling in the mountainous region of Sierra de Galeana and disintegrated on impact.

News of the crash immediately went around the

world. Not surprisingly, the initial reports were sparse and actual facts were obscured by large screaming headlines. But what was certain was that the plane carrying Jenni and her entourage had crashed. It was presumed there were no survivors but until the wreckage was found, nothing could be certain.

It would be nine a.m. Los Angeles time when Pedro Rivera Jr., relaxing in what he explained to reporters was "a beautiful morning' received a call from one of his brothers. "He told me to 'Go see mom because we can't find Jenni's plane. We don't know what happened to her.' I went to my mom's house and then we started getting the news. Then at five p.m. we got the confirmation that Jenni was gone."

It was that glimmer of hope that Jenni's family hung onto in the hours after the reported crash as reporters gathered at the homes of Jenni's mother. Rosa Saavedra, always a deeply religious woman, was quietly hopeful. "If God could make miracles before," she told *La Opinión*, "why wouldn't he do it now with my daughter?" Jenni's father, Don Pedro, also held out hope that the screaming headlines about his daughter's death were merely "press speculation."

Almost immediately after the reports of the crash, Mexican police and soldiers were dispatched to the area where the plane went down to find the wreckage. Their search was aided by helicopters and planes scouring the rugged countryside from above. The consensus was that Jenni's tie to the crash had caused the Mexican government to pull out all the stops in finding the wreckage as quickly as possible.

The world held their collective breath and said silent prayers as the search played out across the

Mexican countryside. Later the same day, numerous outlets, including The Associated Press and Televisa, reported the crashed plane had been found in the state of Nuevo León, near the town of Iturbide in the rugged Sierra Madre Oriental range.

Ruiz Esparza reported to Televisa that "everything points toward the wreckage being from the plane carrying Rivera and six other people." He further reported that the remains and wreckage were scattered over two hundred fifty to three hundred meters and were unrecognizable. Although authorities could not one hundred percent confirm that Jenni was on the plane, the consensus was that she was.

Jenni's father, Don Pedro, put a final note to the tragedy when he told HuffPost Voices quite simply and sadly, "It is true. My daughter is dead."

Almost immediately the ghoulish side of the media reared its ugly head when gruesome, gory footage of the crash site that included images of human remains were mysteriously leaked to the Internet and broadcast around the world. Jenni's family was incensed at these horrifying images being leaked to the world and called for an immediate investigation . It would later be determined that two police officers who had been searching for the wreckage had taken items from the crash site and, allegedly, evidence indicating they had been the ones who leaked the grisly footage was found in their possession. The two officers were instantly arrested. The Mexican government would apologize for the incident and say with more than two million officers in the country, it only took the actions of a few to tarnish their reputation.

In the wake of this horrendous act, the Mexican

government would proceed cautiously in talking about progress being made in finding and identifying the remains. In an interview with Radio Formula, Alejandro Argudin, head of Mexico's Civil Aviation Agency, said "We are in the process of picking up all the fragments and we have to find all the parts. Depending on the weather conditions, it could take us ten days to have a first report."

By Monday, December 10, the grim task of collecting and identifying the remains had begun. The remains of those on board the plane were taken to University Hospital in Monterrey, Mexico, for DNA testing and proper identification. Although the Rivera family was assured they would be notified as soon as the results were confirmed, they were not willing to wait. And so that Monday, Juan, Lupillo, and Gustavo prepared to fly down to Mexico and claim their sister's body.

As the brothers were leaving, a distraught Lupillo told a *New Media Latino* reporter "I'm going to get my sister."

Pedro Rivera Jr. recalled in an enelbrasero.com story that his wife had called Lupillo en route to Mexico to let him know a body had been found, but that it was not Jenni. This gave the family a glimmer of hope. But the reality was that the brothers Rivera knew in their hearts that they were going to Mexico to bring back their sister. Lupillo said as much to *News Media Latino*. "I'm going to pick up the mother of my nieces and nephews. I'm going to pick up the best daughter my mother had."

Once the brothers arrived in Mexico, Nuevo León State Security spokesman Jorge Domene explained to them it would be a few more days before the DNA tests were completed and the identities of the bodies was confirmed. But the brothers Rivera were extremely upset and wanted immediate answers.

Pedro Rivera Jr., waiting back in Los Angeles with his parents, recalled in a *Daily Democrat* feature what happened next. "They did show some pictures to Juan. He took one look and said, 'That's my sister. I don't need to see anymore.' Gus (Gustavo) saw them and said, 'That's my sister.' They didn't even have to wait for the DNA. They all said, 'That's my sister.'"

The anguish displayed on the brother's faces was palpable. But they most likely fought back the tears and, as their actions after the initial identification indicated, they set about doing what had to be done.

In a gesture meant to commemorate Jenni's death, Lupillo, in a story in enelbrasero.com, asked the townspeople of Iturbide to erect a wooden cross to mark Jenni's passing. The city would ultimately comply with his request.

By Thursday, December 13, the entire world had the answer as the DNA tests confirmed that the remains were those of Jenni Rivera.

Pedro Jr. would release the news to assembled media during a press conference. "We have received 100 percent confirmation that my sister has gone to be with the Lord. She is in the presence of God now. They did show pictures of the body to my brothers. It is not the full body."

Once the reality of Jenni's death sunk in, the family faced the torture that was telling Jenni's children that they would never see their mother again. Gustavo told L.A. Remix TV that it was a particularly hard time for the younger children to comprehend.

"The children are very young but they understand. The children see it as their mother still hasn't arrived. It's difficult. It was a huge blow."

Arrangements were immediately made to fly Jenni's body back on a private plane. The plane touched down at Long Beach Airport at seven thirty p.m. It was an eerie tableau. Airport lights blinked in an overcast sky as the plane touched down on the runway and came to a halt. It was surreal. But at the end of the day it was final.

As the plane touched down, Lupillo put out an emotional Tweet. "Jenni. Mission accomplished. You're home."

Jenni Rivera was back in Long Beach. Where it all began.

Word had quickly spread on all aspects of the tragedy, including where and when the plane carrying Jenni's remains would be landing. When the plane taxied to a stop, the brothers Rivera discovered that a small group of fans had gathered just outside the Long Beach Airport gates. As the hearse drove off, those fans first applauded and then offered their heartfelt condolences to the brothers and their family.

The hearse passed silently through the gate and into the dark streets of Los Angeles and was driven with an extensive police escort through the streets of Los Angeles to the Long Beach, California, All Souls Mortuary where she would lie pending funeral arrangements.

Pending some inevitable legal issues, it would be many days before Jenni would finally go to her final rest .

Her brother Pedro, on the day she died, may have summed it up best when he addressed reporters. "Life is like that. We live and we die. We may be sad but when God has the last word, for all of us in our last days, it's time to go.

"And this was the way that Jenni had to go."

CHAPTER TWENTY-TWO

HUMAN NATURE

The memorial and the vigil outside the Lakewood, California, home of the Rivera family kept growing during the five days following the announcement of Jenni's death. In front of the home, flowers, balloons, candles, and posters were stacked in a reverent street memorial. At all hours of the day and night people would drive by and take pictures, or simply stop and share their stories of what Jenni and her music had meant in their lives.

And there were tears. Always tears. And sadness.

Reporters were a constant presence in front of the house, hoping for an appearance of a family member and a tidbit of information that would qualify as a scoop on the Internet. The Spanish-language media was very much a presence during those early days.

During one impromptu interview by Juan in the front of the house, the Spanish news agency EFE got one of the first scraps of information about how the family would handle any observances of Jenni's life when he said, "Soon we will have a ceremony in which we can say goodbye to my sister."

It was a given that any such ceremony would be attended by numerous celebrities in the Latin music world. Controversy was already looming, should Jenni's third and still legally married husband Esteban Loaiza be invited to the public ceremony. With what had come down in the divorce, the family was inclined not to invite him. But Jenni's mother, Rosa, seemed in a forgiving mood and said in a *Qué Más* story that she would be okay with him attending.

"I told him (Esteban) that I loved him. God bless him and give him the peace he has given me."

Pedro Jr., speaking for the rest of the family, reluctantly said in *Qué Más*, "I think he should be at the public ceremony but the private one is another matter."

For his part, Esteban had remained silent after Jenni's death. But in a telephone conversation with the Univision program *Primer Impacto*, he said that out of respect for the Rivera family he would not be attending any public ceremonies but that he did send his heartfelt condolences to the Rivera family. During this interview he also offered his feelings about his late wife.

"I'm going to remember her with all my heart," he said. "I loved her so much and still love her. I'm going to remember her for many reasons but most of all her smile, her love of the stories, and motivation behind her songs and her fans and family."

Amid all the reverence and memories of those first days and weeks after Jenni's death, there would be one blight on the day when her brother Pedro Jr. made a blatant attempt to exploit his sister's death for money. In an article that appeared in *La Prensa*, it was revealed that Pedro Jr. had solicited Jenni's millions of fans to donate $2 million to him for what he said was "Jenni's unrealized dream."

In his plea for money, Pedro said, "Jenni and my sister Rosie wanted to acquire Primer Amor, a church in Long Beach. I'm not sure how this stuff is going to turn out and if God is going to bless us. But my son David told me that Jenni had two million followers on Twitter and if each one can donate a dollar, it would make my sister's dream come true."

What *La Prensa* also reported was that initially, Pedro Jr. had attempted to get the money out of Jenni's assets to buy the church but the Rivera family put their foot down and said no.

Jenni's sudden unexpected death was made all the more heartbreaking by the fact that Jenni and daughter Janney were still estranged and had not yet begun the process of making peace. Janney's friend and reality show co-star RacC (Raquel Córdova) had seen the fallout first hand and sadly told Latina.com how much better it could have been.

"I just wish that certain things could have been different before this happened," she said. "I just wish she and her daughter could have been on good terms. And that's where it hurts me the most. To know that there was unfinished business there. There was an opportunity for Jenni and her daughter to find common ground before her death. That's what hurts me the most out of this whole situation. There was an opportunity for there to be peace but pride and ego and all that got in the way... and now it's too late."

Not surprisingly, shortly after Jenni's death, a number of tribute songs began appearing on the

Internet and various websites. Many saw this as a cynical way of cashing in and getting famous and, in a cynical way, it probably seemed like a good way to get noticed and further one's career.

The Chicago-based group Grupo Dezatados was one of those who seemed to be making the most of the opportunity. The video of their song "Corrido de Jenni Rivera" has had more than two hundred thousand hits on the Internet. The song is being played by several Spanish-language radio stations and there has been a marked increase in interest from booking agents. The song is also available on the band's website for download for 99 cents.

So it seemed a bit incongruous when band member Ismael Hernández told *Billboard*, "It's not about trying to be popular. We simply wanted to sing something in her honor."

A little further up the tribute ladder was Los Angeles-based songwriter Ismael Gallegos, who had worked with such top-flight performers as Pedro Fernández, Los Tigres Del Norte, and Yolanda Del Río, had actually written two tributes to Jenni, "A Una Gran Señora" and "La Diva de la Banda". But rather than rushing a song out, he told *Billboard* he was hoping to record the songs at some point.

People were reacting to Jenni's death in many different ways. And they were being human.

CHAPTER TWENTY-THREE

INVESTIGATION/SPECULATION

The investigation into the plane crash began instantly. But while investigators were doing their due diligence, there was the inevitable outlandish, crazy-making rumor, innuendo, and pure fantasy that often appears in the wake of celebrity-connected tragedy and scandal.

Among those trying for the headlines and their fifteen minutes in the spotlight was an alleged psychic who had wormed his/her way into the Rivera inner circle and was claiming that Jenni was still alive. Another urban myth materialized when an alleged Tweet went out shortly after the crash, claiming the sender was Jenni and that she was asking for help. Those citing Jenni's arrest a few years earlier for attempting to bring large amounts of money across the border, floated the notion that Jenni had, in fact, been approached by the drug cartels to smuggle money into the U.S. for them and, when she allegedly refused, they planted a bomb on the plane.

Once various investigative agencies on both sides of the border began their work, the reality easily eclipsed the fantasy. The first point of attention would be the plane itself and, by association, the two pilots, Miguel Pérez Soto, 78, and Alejandro Torres, 20. In a report that appeared as part of a story by the *Los Angeles Times*, Mexico's Ministry of Communication and Transportation indicated that both pilots were experienced and had valid pilots' licenses. It was also reported that despite his advanced age, Soto was competent and was still allowed to pilot planes.

In an interview with the *Los Angeles Times*, Christian E. Esquino Nuñez, an executive for the company who owned the plane, Starwood Management, said he believes the pilot, Soto, may have had a heart attack or was in some other way incapacitated and that the co-pilot, Torres, was too inexperienced to save the plane. Nuñez further said the Learjet had been well maintained and had undergone a top-to-bottom inspection the previous summer.

Nuñez's defense of the plane's condition would run afoul of U.S. aviation records that indicated that in 2005, the plane sustained considerable damage when the pilot lost control while attempting a landing in Amarillo, Texas, and struck a runway distance marker. Esquino responded by saying the accident in question had been minor and that the plane had flown more than a thousand hours since then without incident.

Nuñez and Starwood Management's credibility would come into question in the coming days when court records released to Univision News indicated Nuñez had a history of illegal activities that included charges that he falsified logbook records on several planes and drug trafficking charges in Florida in 1993, in which he pleaded guilty to conspiracy to possess and distribute cocaine. In the first instance he was found guilty and sentenced to twenty-four months in prison. The drug trafficking charge brought Nuñez a five-year prison sentence.

Taking its cue from the Univision News reports, the Drug Enforcement Administration began their own investigation of Nuñez and Starwood Management that unearthed the fact that two other Starwood Management planes had been seized by DEA agents in the past year, the first in February in Tucson, Arizona, and the second in September in McAllen, Texas. The shaky legal doings of Nuñez would get more bizarre when *El Diario* said they had records that indicated four people were arrested and charged with attempting to use a Starwood Management plane to smuggle family members of former Libyan dictator Muammar Gaddafi into Mexico. Nuñez would serve as a witness at their trial and, ironically, would end up suing to get his plane back.

Like all investigations of this nature, the crash that took the life of Jenni and her entourage had, within a matter of days, blossomed into a major news story all over the world. Any and all documents connected to the plane, the fateful flight, and the plane's owners, as well as objects found at the crash scene, were being investigated by the Mexican Communications and Transportation Secretariat, the Federal Aviation Administration, and the National Transportation Safety Board. The Drug Enforcement Administration was continuing to conduct its own investigation into Nuñez and Starwood Management.

While people were demanding a quick resolution to the investigation, the reality was that a meticulous investigation of the crash would take time. The Mexican Communications and Transportation Secretariat indicated a complete and thorough investigation into the crash could take nine months to a year to complete.

CHAPTER TWENTY-FOUR

EVEN IN DEATH...SCANDAL

Less than a month after Jenni's death, a new scandal came to light when several Mexican-language outlets including Univision, *La Opinión, Reforma*, and Fox News Latino reported that a protected witness had come forward to say Jenni had performed at drug cartel narco festivals in different Mexican cities.

Univision reported that the witness, using the name Jennifer, was at one time a lawyer for the infamous Beltrán Leyva drug cartel, headed up by kingpin "La Barbie." The witness claimed Jenni was among many top musicians who would be hired by a go-between, Jose Carlos Salinas Rodríguez—aka El Charly—to perform at festivals sponsored by and attended by members of drug cartels.

The protected witness also claimed in Univision and *Reforma* stories that she had witnessed Jenni doing cocaine on several occasions and that, on one occasion, La Barbie humiliated the singer by kicking her as a joke.

Reforma reported this witness had made these claims as far back as 2009 when Jenni had been arrested at Mexico's International Airport for allegedly trying to take in excess of $50,000 out of the country.

Some months after that incident, Jenni denied all claims that she was involved with drug trafficking in an interview with *Hola!* But she did admit that sometimes she was in the dark when it came to contracting shows.

"It is true that at times you are not aware of who contracts you for a show," she told *Hola!* "They tell you that you will sing at a certain place and that they will pay you a certain amount of money."

In denying the allegations, she told *Hola!* in no uncertain terms that "She did not want any problems and she would not risk it."

CHAPTER TWENTY-FIVE

THE LETTER AND THE LAW

The aftermath of Jenni Rivera's death could have been messy. In a legal/financial sense there were a lot of loose ends that would, most certainly, have taken years to untangle. Fortunately, Jenni made sure her estate would be handled with dignity in the event of her passing.

Jenni might have had a sense that her time was short, because in October 2012, she wrote a letter and gave it to her sister, Rosie. It was a letter that was only to be made public upon her death.

According to Red Alert Live, the letter turned over the running and distribution of money to her children to her sister. Pedro Rivera Jr. told Red Alert Live "Jenni always had advisors who helped her to work and to make things right."

Outlined in the letter were specific instructions for Rosie to assume the role of CEO of Jenni Rivera Enterprises . Her duties would include the monitoring of all business deals, management of the Jenni Rivera brand, royalty and copyright payments, and all legal issues of a company reportedly worth as much as $25 million. She would also assume guardianship of Jenni's two youngest children, Jenicka and Johnny.

Jenni was specific in the letter as to what should happen to her remains upon her death. She insisted that, no matter the circumstance, that her family retrieve her body and, despite the wishes of her family that she should be cremated, the letter said that she should be buried.

Jenni's foresight in putting somebody she trusted in charge, dotting all the i's and crossing all the t's, probably headed off the majority of potential legal difficulties in the wake of her death. But one question that immediately came to the fore was what rights, if any, third husband Esteban Loaiza might have to the estate.

While divorce papers were filed, Jenni died before the divorce was finalized and so a case could be made that Jenni and Esteban were still legally married at the time of her death. With a pre-nuptial agreement in place, it would suggest Esteban would not be entitled to any money or, at best, whatever the executor of Jenni's estate might consider appropriate. To date, Esteban has not made any legal overtures toward this situation nor has he talked about taking any legal steps. So it remains to be seen.

But while Jenni's letter to Rosie is ironclad, it is inevitable that lawsuits, pending the outcome of the investigation, would most certainly be filed. January 2 brought the first of these lawsuits when the family of Jenni's makeup artist Jacob Yebale, who was among those who perished in the crash, filed a multimillion-dollar lawsuit in Chicago against the owner of Learjet, the owner of the leasing company, and the maintenance company.

Less than a week later, an additional civil lawsuit was filed in Los Angeles by the families of Arturo Rivera, Jorge Vasquez, Mario Pacheco, and Jacob Yebale . This suit was filed against the jet's owners and against Jenni's own company, Jenni Rivera Enterprises, who, the lawsuit claimed in a press conference covered by the Pasadena Star News and other media, may have had a hand in chartering the plane.

Vance Owen, one of the lawyers representing the families told *HuffPost Voices,* "Now we are looking into the possibility that someone within Jenni Rivera's company had something to do with choosing to rent that plane that was a piece of junk."

For the families filing the suit, the decision was nothing if not painful to make. In a conversation with Univision's *El Gordo y La Flaca,* Cynthia Rivera, the sister of Arturo Rivera, who was on the plane, was almost apologetic about filing the suit. "I am not going to profit from this situation. I'm not going to hurt Jenni Rivera's family and her children. This is only part of the investigation. I am not seeking to damage them because they are going through the same thing that I am going through."

Jenni's family had no comment.

In a final indication of the legal frenzy that will, doubtless, drag on for years, the family of the doomed plane's co-pilot, Alejandro Torres, hired an attorney to investigate the crash and to clear their son's name of the charges made in the Los Angeles filed lawsuit that Torres was an inexperienced pilot.

CHAPTER TWENTY-SIX

ALL JENNI, ALL THE TIME

Beyond the tragedy of Jenni Rivera's death, there loomed irony: it took her death for the U.S. media to discover she even existed.

"My impression is that when they suddenly saw her on the cover of all those newspapers, most people were going 'who?'" lamented author Elijah Wald. Wald was particularly incensed and baffled at the press coverage following the crash.

"When I got a phone call saying that Jenni Rivera had died, I immediately went online and it was already on the *New York Times* website. It completely blew my mind. The *Los Angeles Times* never did a feature on her. She was probably the only locally born and raised singer without a movie career to be selling out the sized rooms she was selling out and the *Los Angeles Times* never did a feature on her."

But the *Los Angeles Times* was not the only slight. Just about every news outlet in the U.S. was largely ignorant of who Jenni Rivera was, and was caught totally off guard after the crash. At that point, author and *OC Weekly* editor Gustavo Arellano was being besieged by mainstream press to help them figure out the importance of this singer they never knew existed. Arellano laid out his disdain in an *OC Weekly* blog.

"If only to help (the mainstream news media) correct their pathetic record on reporting on a mega superstar that operated in plain sight under a media that, like usual, didn't bother to pay attention while she was alive because she was a Mexican and popular only to Mexicans. And they never matter unless you can get a diversity grant to cover them."

But while pundits bickered over the media coverage, for the rest of the world it was all about the memory of the singer and her music. Many stations in the Latin community went to either all Jenni music or a large sampling in the days following the accident. U.S. stations for the week following the crash played Jenni Rivera songs 14,700 times, according to *The New York Times*, five times the average number of plays during the previous three weeks.

Mun2 quickly assembled *I Love Jenni* episode marathons. Other Spanish-language television stations rushed to put together documentary-style looks at the life of Jenni. Internet websites were on fire with video and interview clips from back in the day. T-shirts and other clothing with Jenni's image on them were flying out of stores.

Not surprisingly, record sales also exploded. Album sales in the U.S. jumped from six thousand to sixty-four thousand copies in the space of a week. Digital track sales jumped from twelve thousand to eighty-five thousand.

It was revealed early in January that a 40-city

headlining tour that was to begin in 2013 would continue, albeit in an altered state. Espinoza Paz, who was to be Jenni's opening act, would remain with the tour and Gerardo Ortiz would now fill out the bill. The show would go on but it would not be the same.

As the fates would have it, Jenni's label already had a greatest hits/compilation album waiting in the wings. Two days after her death on December 9, the album, "La Misma Gran Señora" (The Same Great Lady) was rush released. While many looked at the release as a deliberate and quickly put together cash-in, the reality was that "La Misma Gran Señora" was a carefully thought-out look at Jenni at her raucous banda best. Culled from albums released over the past seven years, and including her last single, the October release "La Misma Gran Señora", the album was a time capsule, showcasing the fire and charisma that had made Jenni a star. It was a fitting release for the millions of fans who knew her and for those about to discover her.

Jenni's legacy would be further remembered in early February, when it was announced that the late singer had received a total of eleven posthumous nominations for the 2013 *Billboard* Latin Music Awards, whose ceremonies will be held April 25 in Miami, Florida, after this book's release. Those nominations included nods for Artist of The Year, Female Song Artist of the Year, and a double nomination for album of the year for "Joyas Prestadas" and "La Misma Gran Señora".

And the irony was that after years of trying to break into the U.S. English-language market, "La Misma Gran Señora" would debut on the *Billboard* all-album charts at number thirty-eight . Jenni would have appreciated it, perhaps even had a good laugh, before toasting the occasion with a shot of tequila.

CHAPTER TWENTY-SEVEN

REST IN PEACE

In 2003 Jenni wrote a song called "Cuando se muere una dama" (When A Lady Dies) in which she lyrically laid out exactly how she wanted to be remembered. It was a song that painted an upbeat, joyous picture of a funeral wrapped in joy and remembrance, not of sadness. In a perfect world, Jenni already knew how she wanted to be remembered. There were images of beer drinking, hand clapping and dancing and butterflies flying free. In a perfect world, this was the kind of funeral she would have loved to attend. It was the kind of funeral that celebrated life.

Jenni would have been happy that her family and friends had taken the song to heart.

The family's plans for the memorial celebration were well thought-out. Tickets for the event were scaled to one dollar so Jenni's fans, most of limited means, would have the opportunity to attend. The tickets were made available at noon on December 18, 2012, and reportedly sold out within the hour. No press was allowed in the event but along with the thousands who did not attend, they had access to a worldwide streaming video of the ceremony. Those in attendance were also given the opportunity to make a donation to the Jenni Rivera Love Foundation.

A packed Gibson Amphitheater in Los Angeles. Family pictures rotating in and out of a warmly lit background. Superstar singers. A smoking banda band. A red ruby casket sitting center stage behind a mass of white flowers. Family and friends and just plain folks. Behind the coffin a microphone standing stately, pristine, unused.

Waiting for the spirit of Jenni to arrive and get this memorial started.

December 19 was the day chosen by Jenni's family. In keeping with the way Jenni lived her life, what they were calling A Celestial Graduation, a time to remember, a time to mourn, and ultimately a time to rejoice and remember the spirit that Jenni brought to her forty-three years on this earth. Inside, a packed house of 6,100. Outside, several hundred more.

There was music, songs that Jenni made her own, sung by such legendary Latin performers as Ana Gabriel, Olga Tañón, and Joan Sebastian. Through the tears and the sadness, Jenni's father, Don Pedro, serenaded the well-wishers and supporters with a stirring rendition of a song he had written for his daughter, "La Diva de la Banda."

There was not a dry eye in the house when family members and important people in Jenni's life came forward to express their feelings of sadness and inspiration.

Jenni's youngest son, Johnny, brought the already anguished crowd to tears when he said, "Mama, I've been crying so much the last few days. I miss you so much. I hope you are taking care of my dad and I hope he is taking care of you."

Jenni's manager, Pete Salgado, was equally heartfelt in his memories. "Jenni made it okay for women to be who they are. Jenni also made it okay to be from nothing with the hopes of being something."

Jenni's brother, Pedro Rivera Jr., couched his remarks in religious tones. "My sister Jenni died in a plane accident. But it was not an accident. God has a purpose for all of us and God let us borrow Jenni for forty-three years and let us enjoy her."

The very public celebration of Jenni Rivera's life was over. On December 31 it was time for the Rivera family to be alone with their thoughts and prayers as they laid their daughter, sister, and mother to rest. The private ceremony, held at All Souls Cemetery in Long Beach, was a study in introspection as the family took stock in what Jenni Rivera's life had meant to them and so many millions of others. The family stood with the casket that would soon go to ground one last time. An emotional Lupillo hoisted a beer and sang a final song to the spirit of his sister.

It would remain for Jenni's daughter, Janney to put the life and career of her mother in the best possible perspective.

"My mother was perfectly imperfect."

EPILOGUE

A NEW BEGINNING

Rosie Rivera Tweeted the announcement in January. She was eleven weeks pregnant.

"At the doctor's appointment. Officially 11 weeks. Heard our baby's heartbeat. Strong. Fast. On tempo. Thank you lord."

A month after her sister's death. There would be a new life—and a new beginning.

DISCOGRAPHY

LA MISMA GRAN SEÑORA
(2012)

SONGS: La Misma Gran Señora, Resulta, La Gran Señora, Ya Lo Sé, Por Qué No Le Calas?, Hermano Amigo, Trono Caído, Besos y Copas, Por un Amor Cucurrucucu Paloma, Qué Me Vas a Dar, No Vas A Creer, No Me Pregunten Por Él, Ovarios.

JOYAS PRESTADAS (POP)
(2011)

SONGS: A Cambio de Que, A Que No Le Cuentas, Así Fue, Basta Ya, Como Tu Mujer, Detrás de Mi Ventana, Lo Siento Mi Amor, Que Ganas de No Verte Más, Resulta, Señora Porque Me Gusta, A Morir.

JOYAS PRESTADAS (BANDA)
(2011)

SONGS: A Combio de Que, A Qué No Le Cuentas, Así Fue, Untitled, Como tu Mujer, Detrás de Mi Ventana, Lo Siento Mi Amor, Que Ganas de No Verte Más, Resulta, Señora Porque Me Gusta, A Morir.

LA GRAN SEÑORA EN VIVO
(2010)

SONGS: Mi Vida Loca 2, Cuanto Te Debo, Cuando Me Acuerdo de Ti, Tu Camisa Puesta, Chuper Amigos,

Dama Divina, Ni Me Viene De Mi Va, Como Tu Mujer, Por Qué No Le Calanas?, La Gran Señora, Viene De Mi Va, Como Tu Mujer, Por Que No Le Calanas?, La Gran Señora, Ya Lo Sé, Qué Me Vas A Dar?, Inolvidale, Mudanzas, Él (banda version), Él (album version).

LA GRAN SEÑORA
(2009)

SONGS: Yo Soy Mujer, Por Qué No Calas, Before The Next Teardrop Falls, Déjame Volver Contigo, La Cara Bonita, SONGS: Yo Soy Mujer, Por Qué No Calas, Before The Next Teardrop Falls, Déjame Volver Contigo, La Cara Bonita, Ya Lo Sé, Ni Princess Ni Esclara, No Llega El Olvido, Amaneciste Conmigo, La Escalera, La Gran Señora, Amarga Navidad, Estaré Contigo Cuando Triste Estés.

JENNI: SUPER DELUXE
(2009)

SONGS: Chuper Amigos, Culpable O Innocente, Envuélvete, Tu Camisa Puesta, Con Él, La Primera Piedra, Fraude (Toda Un Majer), Vale La Pena, Mudanzas, Lo Pasado Pasado, La Rementada, Ovarios.

JENNI
(2008)

SONGS: Chuper Amigos, Culpable o Innocente, Envuélvete, Tu Camisa Puesta, Ni Me Viene Ni Me Va, Con Él, Cuando Me Acuerdo, De Ti, Fraude,

Trono Caído, Vale La Pena, La Cama, Mudanzas, Culpable o Innocente (pop version), La Primera Piedra.

EXITOS CON BANDA MARIACHI NORTEÑO
(2008)

SONGS: Ando Que Me Lleva, Yo Vendo Unos Ojos Negros, La Captura Del Ceja Guera, Las Cinco Mulas, Los Dos Hermanos, Valente Rojas, El Michoacano, Camisa De Juera, Sucedió En La Barranca, Arroz Del Mismo Costal.

LA DIVA EN VIVO
(2007)

SONGS: Sufriendo a Solas, Popurri: Por un Amor/Cucurrucucu Paloma, La Differencia, Innocente, Pobre Amiga, Paloma Negra, Libro Abierto, Me Siento Libre, Brincos Dieras, Qué Ma Vas a Dar, De Contrabando, La Mentada Contestada, Navidad Sin Ti.

MI VIDA LOCA
(2007)

SONGS: Intro: Esúchame, Mi Vida Loca 2, Intro: Mi Primer Amor, Ahora Que Estuviste Lejos, Intro: Look At Me Now, Mírame, Intro: Nuestro Padre Sangre de Indio, Intro: Qué Bonito Se Siente, La Sopa del Bebe, Intro: La Manutención, Cuánto Te Debo, Intro: Equivocada, I Will Survive, Intro: Mi Madre y Yo, Déjame Vivir, Intro: Mis Hermanos y Yo, Hermano Amigo, Intro: Pimienta Especies, Inolvidable, Intro: Madre y Padre, Sin Capitán, Intro: Metamorfosis,

Mariposa de Barrio, Gracias...Mi Gente.

BESOS Y COPAS DESDE HOLLYWOOD
(2006)

SONGS: Por un Amor/Cucurrucucu Paloma, Juro Que Nunca Volveré, Querida Socia, Soy Madre Soltera, La Tequilera, Homenage Mi Madre, Cuando Yo Quería Ser Grande, Las Mismas Costumbres, Amiga Si Lo Ves, Que Se Te Olvida, Que Mi Vas a Dar, Besos y Copas, Mil
Heridas.

EN VIVO DESDE HOLLYWOOD
(2006)

SONGS: Parrandera, Rebelde y Atrevida, La Chacalosa, Popurri: Reina de Reinas/Rosita Alvirez/Mi Vida Loca, Las Malandrinas, Popurri: Como Tu Decidas/Cuando Yo Quería, Has de Volver, Popurri: Wasted Days And Wasted Nights/Angel Baby, Chicana Jalisciense, Se Marcho, Se las Voy a Dar a Otro, Cuando Abra los Ojos, El Nopal, Popurri: A Escondidas/Hacer El Amor con Otro.

PARRANDERA, REBELDE Y ATREVIDA
(2005)

SONGS: Parrandera, Rebelde y Atrevida, Qué Me Vas a Dar, De Contrabando, Brincos Dieras, La Mentada Contestada, No Vas a Creer, Imbécil, No Me Pregunten, Por Él, Que Se Te Alvido, Jefa de Jefas, Me Siento Libre, Cuando Muere una Dema.

SIMPLEMENTE...LA MEJOR
(2004)

SONGS: Querida Socia, Las Malandrinas, Se Las Voy a Dar a Otro, Cuando Abras los Ojos, Chicana Jalisciense, Que Me Entierren con la Banda, Se Marcho, Mi Vida Loca,Tristeza Pasajera, Angel Baby, Reina de Reinas, La Chacalosa, Las Mismas Costumbres (new version), Amiga Si Lo Vas (new version), Simplemente...La Mejor (new version), Las Mismas Costumbres (nortenaversion), Amiga Si Lo Ves (nortena version), Amiga Si Lo Ves (pop version).

HOMENAJE A LAS GRANDES
(2003)

SONGS: La Popa Sin Catsup, A Escondidas, Por Un Amor, Cucurrucucu Paloma, Ese Hombre, Juro Que Nunca Volver,La Tequilera, Ahora Veugo a Verte, Hacer el Amor con Otro, Homenage Mi Madre, Where Did Our Love Go, La Papa Sin Catsup (nortena version), A Escondidas (nortena version), Juro Que Nunca Volver (nortena version), Hacer El Amor con Ontro (norteña version).

SE LAS VOY A DAR A OTRO
(2001)

SONGS: Angel Baby, No Vas a Jugar, Cuando Abras los Ojos, El Nopal, Tristeza Pasajera, Chicano Jalisciense, Ni Te Esposa Ni Ti Amante Ni Tu Amiga, Se las Voy a Dar a Otro, Se Marcho, Escandalo.

DEJATE AMAR
(2001)

SONGS: Una Noche Me Embriague, Dejate Amar, Mi Vida Loca, Querida Socia, Y Te Me Vas, Madre Soltera, El Ultimo Adios, Agente de Veritas, Cuando Yo Quiera Que Has de Volver, Wasted Days And Wasted Nights.

QUE ME ENTIERREN CON LA BANDA
(2000)

SONGS: Que Me Entierren Con La Banda, Como Tu Decides, Que Con Rayo Te La Parta, Las Malandrinas, Son Habladas, Rosita Alvrez, Mariana Te Accordaras, Solo Se De Amor, Sinaloa Princesa Nortena, Ni Estanda Loca, La Reina del Palenque.

REYNA DE REYNAS
(1999)

SONGS: Reyna de Reynas, El Desquite, El Orguilo de Mi Padre, Popurri de Chelo, Los Traficantes, La Reyna Es el Rey, La Martina El Bato Gacho, La Maestra del Contrabando, Salúdame al la Tuya, Las Cachanillas.

SI QUIERES VERME LLORAR
(1999)

SONGS: Brincos Dieras, Perdonar Es Olvidar, Llanto Rojo, Lagrimas Sudory Sangre, La Puerta, de Alcala, Su Quires Verme Llorar, Vivir Sin Tu Carvio,

Nosotros, Como Vivir Sin Verte, Tonto, Yo Te
Agradezco.

LA CHACALOSA
(1995)

SONGS: La Chacalosa, Tambien las Mujeres Pueden,
Libro Abiesto, Cruz De Madera, Emlargame Ami, Por
Una Pencilla Vieja, Si Tu Bensabas, La Perra
Contrabandista, Cuando el Destino, Mi Gusto Es, Ni
Mc Desbes Ni Te Debo.

SOMOS RIVERA
(1995)

SONGS: Somos Rivera, Alma Enamorada, Amor
Prohibido, Juan Guardado, Me Espera El Camino, De
Vista Al Mundo, Recuerdos de Cullican, Cuento
Perdido, Magda Olilia, Antojos Nobles.

SOURCES

I want to thank author/music historian Elijah Wald for his time and insightful interviews. His first-hand knowledge of the Narcocorrido, Norteño, Banda, Mariachi, and Ranchera genres and experiences and observations interviewing Jenni and her family were gold.

BOOKS: *Narcocorrido: A Journey into the Music of Drugs, Guns, and Guerrillas.* By Elijah Wald.

TELEVISION: L.A. Remix TV, *Cristina, Aquí y Ahora,* CNN, *El Gordo y La Flaca,* Máximo TV, Channel 62 News, Univision, Televisa Chapultepec, Paparazzi TV, Escándalo TV, Primer Impacto, Krist TV.

WEBSITES: Mysanantonio.com, Latin American Herald Tribune.com, Ladivadelabanda.net, Everything Explained @Jenni_Rivera/, Jenni Rivera Music.com, New Media Latino.com, Huffingtonpost.com, Northcountytimes.com, Que Mas, Mamaslatinas.com, OpenYourEyes.com, Spanishtown.com, Latingossip.com, Metrolyrics.com, Latinovoices.com, Terra.com, Latina.com,Glaad.org, Latin Heat.com,CNN.com, NBClatino.com, Colorlines.com, AMP CBSlocal.com, Latino.foxnews.com, Big Story,app.org, Huffpostvoices.com, Dallasnews.com, Hispanicallyspeakingnews.com, NPR.com, Racialicious.com, Perezhilton.com, VOXXI.com, BBC.com, Invision.com, YahooNews.com,

FlightAware.com, HogarAlDia.com, ABCnews.go.com, 29-95.com, Enelbrasero.com, CNS.com, Radio Formula.com, MTV News.com, Examiner.com, LALateNews.com, Insurance Journal.com, Guide live.com.

NEWSPAPERS: *San Antonio News Express, Los Angeles Times, Orange County Weekly, Associated Press, El Paso Express, The New York Times, The Hollywood Reporter, La Opinión, El Diario, Reforma, Houston Chronicle, New York Daily News, Long Beach Post, Pasadena Star News, Arizona Republic, Long Beach Press Telegram, The Press Enterprise, Los Angeles Daily News, La Prensa.*

MAGAZINES: *Billboard, People, People En Español, The Nation, Parade.*

ABOUT THE AUTHORS

Marc Shapiro has covered film, television and music for national and international newspapers and magazines for 25 years. He is the author of *The Secret Life of EL James, J.K. Rowling: The Wizard behind Harry Potter, Justin Bieber: The Fever!* and other bestselling celebrity biographies.

Charlie Vázquez is a Bronx-born journalist, novelist, poet and cultural producer. The author of two novels and a collection of bilingual poetry. he has edited two anthologies of new Latino literature. He has lectured at universities and cultural institutions in the United States, Mexico and Puerto Rico and is the New York City coordinator for Puerto Rico's "The Word/Festival de la Palabra."

Made in the USA
Monee, IL
07 July 2026

56552455R00105